Contents

Introduction

Preschoolers are a delightful age group to teach! For these little ones, so many things are new and exciting. It is the perfect time to make the Bible come to life for this highly imaginative age.

When working with preschoolers, below are some of the things you can expect.

Preschool children:

- Can speak in sentences of five to six words
- Like to tell stories
- Can correctly names some colors
- Understand the concept of counting and may know a few numbers
- Understand the concept of same and different
- Engage in fantasy play
- Are interested in new experiences
- Cooperate with other children
- Can write some letters
- Begin to use scissors purposefully
- Like to sing silly songs, make up goofy words and start rhyming
- Can share, cooperate, be helpful and take turns

When writing this book, I've kept all these things in mind as I have developed activities that are appropriate for preschoolers' current skill levels and will also help them to grow just a bit more.

Instant Bible Lessons

for PRESCHOOLERS

26 LESSONS Reproducible!

A is for **Adam**

B is for **Bible**

C is for **Caleb**

D is for **Daniel**

A to Z THRU THE BIBLE

 HENDRICKSON PUBLISHERS ROSE KiDZ®

INSTANT BIBLE LESSONS FOR PRESCHOOLERS: A TO Z THRU THE BIBLE

RoseKidz® is an imprint of
Rose Publishing, LLC
140 Summit Street
P.O. Box 3473
Peabody, Massachusetts 01961-3473
www.hendricksonrose.com

All Scripture quotations, unless otherwise indicated, are taken from the Holy Bible, New International Reader's Version®, NIrV® Copyright © 1995, 1996, 1998, 2014 by Biblica, Inc.™ Used by permission of Zondervan. All rights reserved worldwide. www.zondervan.com. The "NIrV" and "New International Reader's Version" are trademarks registered in the United States Patent and Trademark Office by Biblica, Inc.™

ISBN: 9781628627435

RoseKidz® reorder number R50017

RELIGION / Christian Ministry / Children

Printed in the United States of America

01 5.2018.VP

We know variety is an integral part of working with kids, and you'll find plenty of different activities to keep kids engaged no matter what their preferred learning style is. In this book, I have included simple stories, games, crafts, pretend play and much more.

Learning the alphabet is a thrilling milestone for many children (and their parents!) and we wanted to use this special time to help introduce key Bible stories to preschool kids. Throughout the book, each chapter focuses on one letter of the alphabet along with a coordinating story from the Bible. Not only will children learn about many of the Biblical accounts Christians build our faith on, they will engage in fun projects and tasks along the way. As they continue to grow, we hope that each time they review the alphabet; they will remember these lessons from the Bible.

This book is a perfect resource for the preschool classroom at your church as well as a great book to have on the shelf at home. With the vivid illustrations and easy to do activities, it would serve as an excellent starter book for the homeschooling family. We hope that it will help you to introduce many of the amazing accounts in the Bible while learning and growing academically at the same time.

Keep on serving the Lord!

Lindsey Whitney

GrowingKidsMinistry.com

How to Use This Book

This book is arranged in alphabetical order. Each chapter focuses on one letter of the alphabet as well as a specific passage in the Bible. Before you teach or share the lessons with your preschool group, take time to read through the passage in your own Bible (and maybe even the chapters before and after it) so that you will understand the story in its context and be prepared for any questions the kids might have.

The **INTRODUCTION** in each chapter will help you to understand the story and any important background information you might need to teach.

The **OPENING ACTIVITY** is an open-ended activity that can be used with early arrivers or as a transition activity between free play and the lesson. It is designed to be hands-on and will get children thinking about the story ahead.

The **BIBLE STORY** itself is intended to be read like a favorite story. Show the picture to the children as you read and allow them to ask questions as you go. The language is simple to help preschoolers understand.

The **I WONDER** section is (hopefully) a contemplative break in the otherwise highly busy preschool classroom. It is a chance for children and leaders to wonder out loud about various elements of the story. Allow children to talk freely without interjecting too much.

Many of the questions do not have a clear "right or wrong" answer but are deliberately designed to encourage children to think deeper about the Bible, the character of God, and how the people in the story were feeling.

No lesson book would be complete without a bit of review! In the ALPHABET REVIEW section, encourage children to name the letters in the alphabet and their matching Bible story. If you have a schedule that allows it, you may wish to select a favorite activity from each letter and have a complete review session every eight weeks or so. This will help children remember what they have learned and will provide them with a chance to participate again in the activities that brought them the most joy.

Each chapter contains OPTIONAL EXTRA ACTIVITIES that coordinate with the letter and Biblical account. These activities were built around key preschool skills such as identifying shapes, counting, working with others, and gross-motor-skill development. The skills needed for each activity are listed to help you plan for your particular group.

We have included PRINTING PRACTICE and a COLORING PAGE in each chapter because handwriting and fine-motor development are integral to the preschool experience. Both will help little hands build their endurance as well as reinforce what they have learned during the lesson.

Preschool children are a bucket of fun to be around and it is our hope and prayer that this resource will help you enjoy this special time and give you a clear roadmap for introducing a few of the amazing stories from the Bible.

ENJOY!

Fun Songs

Sing these fun songs with kids during clean-up time, while waiting for parents to pick up children, or anytime you need a time-filler.

CLEAN UP SONG

To the Tune of "London Bridge"

It's time to clean our room today.
Clean our room.
Clean our room.
It's time to clean our room today,
All God's children.

GOD LOVES CHILDREN

To the Tune of "Three Blind Mice"

God loves children. (Repeat 4 times.)
He loves us more than we can know.
He gave us the Bible so we could know.
That God loves children!

JONAH'S SONG

To the Tune of "London Bridge"

Jonah was swallowed by a fish,
By a fish,
By a fish,
Jonah was swallowed by a fish.
Swallowed whole!

A Is for Adam

Genesis 2

INTRODUCTION

God created the earth and everything in it. He created the sky, the stars, the moon and the sun. He made the plants, the birds, and the fish in the sea. He also made humans. The first human God every created was a man named Adam. God placed Adam in a beautiful garden and gave him fruit to eat. God also created a woman to be a helper and companion to Adam. Together, they were to take care of the garden and the animals God had created.

OPENING ACTIVITY

LET'S MAKE SOMETHING!

WHAT YOU NEED

- Play dough

WHAT YOU DO

1. Pass out a fist-sized lump of play dough to each child.

2. Children make something special with their play dough. (See suggestions in the box.)

3. When everyone is done, children show and tell the group what they made.

IDEAS FOR THINGS TO MAKE

- Ball
- Snake
- Cat
- Tree
- House
- Cookie
- Etc.

WHAT YOU SAY

You guys did a great job making something! Do you like playing with play dough? Can you imagine making something that actually was alive? Of course, we can't do that, but God can! God created all things, and he didn't even use play dough to do it! God is powerful and strong. Today, we're going to talk about how God made something very special—the first man on Earth. His name was Adam and God loved him very much. Let's find out more!

THE BIBLE STORY

Genesis 2:1–24

Long ago, there was nothing on Earth. Everything was dark and empty. Then, God made all kinds of things!

It was very exciting. God made the sun and the stars, the animals and plants, and the fish and birds. God loved all the things that he made, but he wasn't done!

God also made humans. The first person God made was a man named Adam. God took some dust from the ground and created Adam. Then, God placed him in a beautiful garden.

In this garden, there were many trees that gave Adam food. Adam could eat from any of the trees except for one— the tree of knowing good and evil.

Soon, God could tell that Adam needed a friend, so God created a woman named Eve. Adam and Eve were happy in the garden. They were friends with God and God loved them very much.

Day 1 · Day 2 · Day 3

6 Days of Creation

Day 4 · Day 5 · Day 6

I WONDER . . .

After the story, read these "wonder" statements and questions out loud to your group. Encourage children to respond.

- I wonder why God made so many different kinds of animals. Let's name different animals!
- I wonder why God made humans. Why do you think God made humans?
- I wonder what kinds of fruits were in the garden. How many fruit can you name?
- What do you wonder about the story?

ALPHABET REVIEW

After each lesson, take a few minutes to go over the letters you have recently learned and the Bible stories that go with them. You can use the coloring pages from each week as a timeline and to aid in reviewing.

OPTIONAL EXTRA ACTIVITIES

PLAY DOUGH LETTERS

WHAT YOU NEED

- Play dough

WHAT YOU DO

1. Give each child a fist-sized lump of play dough.
2. Children form letters with their play dough.

TEACHING TIP: To help children with the shapes, find free play dough mats online by searching "play dough alphabet mats."

PRESCHOOL SKILLS

- Letter recognition
- Fine-motor skills

FRUIT TREES

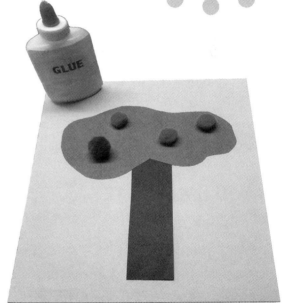

WHAT YOU NEED

- Construction paper in green, brown, and white
- Scissors
- Glue
- Small pom-poms

WHAT YOU DO

1. Children cut a cloud shape from the green construction paper to make a tree top.
2. Children cut a rectangle shape from the brown construction paper to make a tree trunk.
3. Children glue shapes to the white construction paper to form a tree.
4. Children glue the pom-poms onto the top of tree to represent fruit.

PRESCHOOL SKILLS

- Identifying shapes
- Fine-motor skills
- Scissor skills

GOD MADE ME

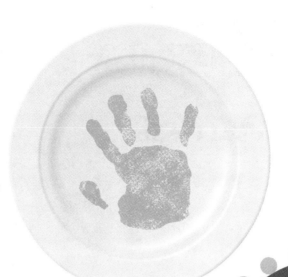

WHAT YOU NEED

- Paintbrush
- Washable paint
- White paper plates (not Styrofoam)
- Markers

Optional

- Smocks

WHAT YOU DO

OPTIONAL: Children put on smocks or paint shirts.

1. Use paintbrush to gently brush paint onto each child's hands.

2. Children press their hands down onto the top part of a paper plate. Make sure children leave room at the bottom for Step 3 below.

3. Below the hands, print "God made the world and God made (Brianna)." Set aside to dry.

PRESCHOOL SKILLS

- Recognizing name in print
- Identifying body parts

Optional

- Putting on a smock or shirt

NAME THAT ANIMAL

WHAT YOU NEED

- Animal Cards, page 15
- Scissors or paper cutter

Optional

- Laminator

WHAT YOU PREPARE

Copy and cut apart Animal Cards.

WHAT YOU DO

One at a time, hold up each card and ask children to name the animal.

WHAT YOU SAY

Wow! Can you imagine naming all the animals on Earth? That's exactly what Adam did at the beginning of time. What a hard job that must have been. What hard jobs do you do?

BONUS IDEA: Make extra copies of Animal Cards so children can play Concentration.

PRESCHOOL SKILLS

- Working in groups
- Naming common animals

Optional

- Exercising memory

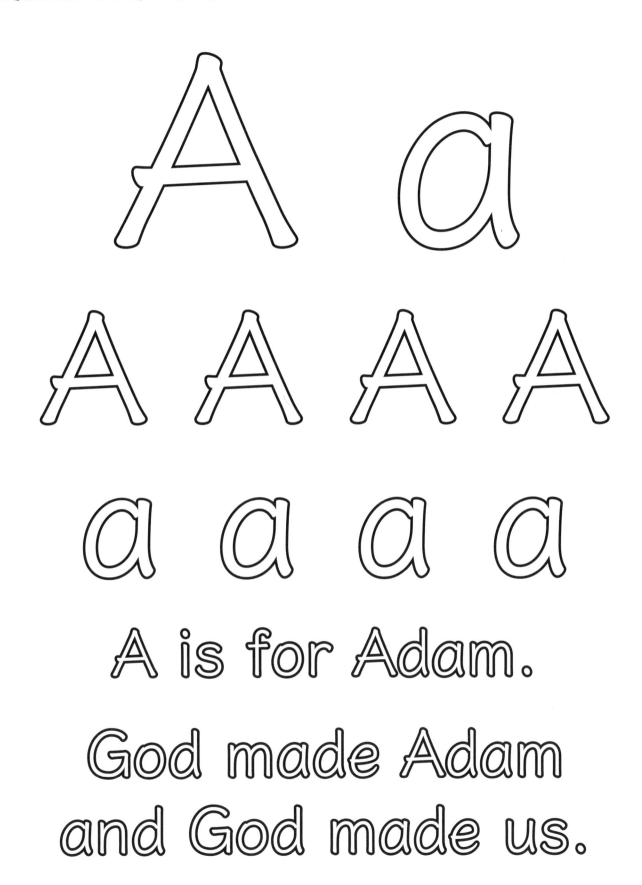

A a

A A A A

a a a a

A is for Adam.

God made Adam
and God made us.

A is for Adam.

God made a man named Adam,
Standing strong and tall.
Then Adam named the animals,
Both the big and the small.

ANIMAL CARDS

Lion	Elephant	Horse	Pig
Cat	Eagle	Butterfly	Shark
Cow	Sheep	Fish	Worm
Raccoon	Giraffe	Fox	Monkey
Dog	Hamster	Rabbit	Tiger
Wolf	Alligator	Camel	Flamingo

B Is for Bible

Psalm 119

INTRODUCTION

God gave us the Bible to show us his plan for the world. Even though Adam and Eve (the first people on Earth) lived in a paradise, they did not remain there for long. Because they disobeyed God, they brought sin into the world. God cannot be near sin and so he made a plan to save us from the sin in the world. The Bible tells us all about that plan. The Bible also tells us how to live as children of God. It shows us a clear path for living life God's way. David, the author of Psalm 119, delighted in God's word and took time to read the Scriptures regularly (Psalm 119:14–16). We should do the same.

OPENING ACTIVITY

WALK THIS WAY

WHAT YOU NEED

- Bean bag or cone

WHAT YOU PREPARE

Place the bean bag on one side of the room. If the room is empty, place a few chairs or obstacles in the middle of the playing area.

WHAT YOU DO

1. Ask for a volunteer. Child stands against the wall on one side of the room.

2. Give the child clear instructions to get closer to the bean bag: Take one step forward, take two steps to the right, take a big step to the left, etc. Purposefully lead the child away from bean bag from time to time.

3. When child reaches the bean bag, lead group to celebrate.

4. Repeat with additional volunteers as time and interest allow.

WHAT YOU SAY

In this game, we could clearly see our goal, but life isn't always like that. Sometimes our parents (or teachers) ask us to do something that we don't entirely understand. Sometimes we just have to trust and obey. The Bible is filled with people who trusted God and obeyed him, even when it didn't always make sense. God has a good plan for our lives and the world. Often, he only gives us one direction at a time—just like I did in this game. We can find directions for living God's way in the Bible.

THE BIBLE STORY

Psalm 119

The Bible is a very special book. It is not like any other book on Earth. It comes directly from God.

God told people what to write in the Bible. God wants us to know all about his plan and how much he loves us. God tells us how to live in the Bible. The Bible is full of amazing things!

David was a man who lived long ago. David was a shepherd for a long time and then he became a king.

David loved the Bible. He knew that a person could learn the right thing to do by reading God's Word, the Bible. David regularly read the Bible. He thanked God for such an amazing book. David said that the Bible was more precious than riches.

This is true. The Bible is a special gift to us from God.

I WONDER . . .

After the story, read these "wonder" statements and questions out loud to your group. Encourage children to respond.

- I wonder why God gave us the Bible. What do you do when you want to tell someone something?
- I wonder what your favorite story is from the Bible. What's your favorite story, (Siena)?
- I wonder how many people have a Bible in their home. What could we do if someone didn't have a Bible in their home?
- What do you wonder about the Bible?

ALPHABET REVIEW

Take a few minutes to go over the letters you have recently learned and the Bible stories that go with them. You can use the coloring pages from each week as a timeline and to aid in reviewing.

OPTIONAL EXTRA ACTIVITIES

BLOCK MATCH UP

WHAT YOU NEED

- Letter Squares, page 23
- Sheets of white and colored paper
- Scissors or paper cutter

WHAT YOU PREPARE

Copy Letter Squares on white paper, making one for each child. On colored paper, make additional copies of Letter Squares, and cut into individual squares. Place letter squares where children can easily reach them.

WHAT YOU DO

1. Give each child a copy of the white Letter Squares sheet.

2. Children place the colored letter squares on the matching letters on their paper to spell the words.

3. Read the words for the children after they complete each word.

PRESCHOOL SKILLS

- Independent play
- Letter recognition
- Hand-eye coordination
- Matching objects

I LOVE THE BIBLE!

WHAT YOU NEED

- Heart-shaped hole punch (available online or at craft stores)
- Marker
- Construction paper
- Glue sticks

WHAT YOU PREPARE

In the center of a sheet of construction paper, print "I love the Bible." Prepare one paper for each child. On additional sheets of construction paper, punch out at least ten hearts for each child.

WHAT YOU DO

1. Read the words to the children and remind children of what an amazing book the Bible is as they glue hearts all around the outside edge of their papers.

ALTERNATE IDEAS: Use computer software and a printer to print "I love the Bible." on sheets of paper instead of writing by hand. Instead of punching out heart shapes for children to glue, use heart-shaped stickers.

- - - - - - - - - - - - - -

BOOKS OF THE BIBLE

WHAT YOU NEED

- Bible

WHAT YOU SAY

Open your Bible to the Table of Contents. **This is a list of the books of the Bible. When I say the name of a Bible book, we'll all jump high in the air! If I say a word that is NOT a book in the Bible, we'll all sit down.**

WHAT YOU DO

1. Play several rounds, sometimes saying a book of the Bible and jumping, and sometimes saying other words and sitting down.

TEACHING TIP: This is a fun way to introduce the books of the Bible. Be sure you LEAD children in their responses. Jump and sit with them. Though it is not impossible, it is highly improbable that a preschooler would know any books of the Bible.

PRESCHOOL SKILLS

- Identifying heart shape
- Fine-motor skills

Optional
- Identify colors

PRESCHOOL SKILLS

- Gross-motor skills
- Listening and responding

I SPY JAR

WHAT YOU NEED

- Small objects (toy figures, small cars, buttons, coins, tiny animals, bouncy balls, erasers, game pieces, puzzle pieces, hair clips, etc.)
- Mason jar with lid
- Rice or small beads
- Sheet of paper
- Pencil or pen

WHAT YOU PREPARE

Place the small objects inside of the jar. Fill the rest of the jar with rice or small beads. On sheet of paper, make a list of the objects you put inside the jar.

WHAT YOU DO

1. Gather children around you and name one of the objects you hid inside the jar.
2. Children look in the jar as it is rotated to see if they can spot the hidden object.
3. Play several rounds as time and interest allow.

WHAT YOU SAY

There are a lot of cool things hidden inside this jar! The Bible is also filled with good things. There are amazing true stories, poems, verses to help us when we are afraid, and verses to help us know the right thing to do. It is a like a book full of hidden treasures!

PRESCHOOL SKILLS

- Working in groups
- Object permanence

B b

B B B B

b b b b

B is for Bible.

God gave us the Bible.

Instant Bible Lessons for Preschoolers: A to Z Thru the Bible

COLORING PAGE

B is for Bible.

God gave us the Bible and it is true.
The Bible helps us know just what to do.
God loves us so much, as you can see.
He sent his Son, Jesus, to save you and me.

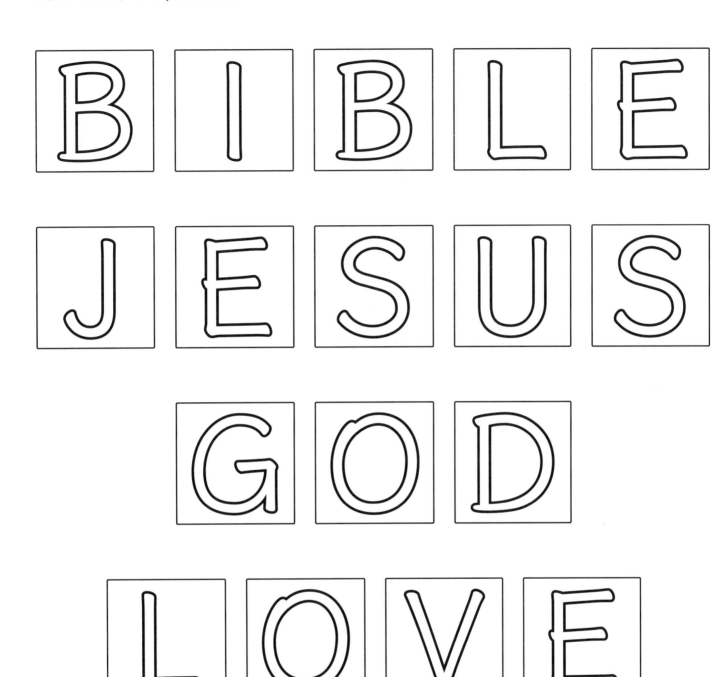

C Is for Caleb

Numbers 13–14

INTRODUCTION

There were many times in the Bible where God gave what seemed like an impossible task to his followers. In one case, God led his people to a wonderful land filled with good food and fields for planting. It was called Canaan and it was a special land that God had promised to his people. When the people arrived at the land, they went in to explore. Twelve men explored the land and ten were so afraid of the people who lived there that they asked to go back to Egypt (where they had previously lived as slaves). Only Caleb and Joshua trusted God. They knew with God's protection and strength, they could win the battle and live in the good land.

OPENING ACTIVITY

BIG AND SMALL

WHAT YOU NEED

- Variety of toy people

WHAT YOU DO

1. Place the toy people in a pile in the middle of the floor or table.

2. Children put toy people in size order with the smallest person on one end and the tallest person on the other.

WHAT YOU SAY

In our true story today, God's people were moving to the wonderful place God promised would be their new home. But the people were afraid! There were giants living in the land (Numbers 13:32–33)**. If these toy people were a part of this story, which ones would be God's people? Which ones would be the giants living in the land? Even though the giants living in the land were big, God is more powerful. Caleb trusted God even when the rest of God's people did not.**

THE BIBLE STORY

Numbers 13–14

God has a special plan for his people. Long ago, God wanted to give his people a new land to live in. He called this the Promised Land. It was beautiful and good for growing food.

When God's people got to their new land, they found a bunch of grapes so big, it took two men to carry it! But they also became very afraid. There were giants living in the land! God's people did not think they could win a battle against them. Many of the people wanted to run away. But there were two men who trusted God and wanted to obey him.

Caleb was one of the men who trusted God. Caleb told the people, "We should go and move into this new land. We can do it!"

The people did not listen to Caleb. They did not trust God. Caleb knew that God is powerful and strong. He trusted God and we can trust God too.

Because Caleb trusted God, he was later allowed to live in the special Promised Land when many of the other people were not. Caleb trusted in God's plan and was rewarded for his obedience. We can trust in God's plan too.

I WONDER . . .

After the story, read these "wonder" statements and questions out loud to your group. Encourage children to respond.

- I wonder what kinds of things the people saw in the new land. What do you think they saw?
- I wonder why the people were so afraid. When are times kids your age feel afraid?
- I wonder if the people were sorry they did not listen to God. When do you feel sorry?
- What do you wonder about our Bible story?

ALPHABET REVIEW

Take a few minutes to go over the letters you have recently learned and the Bible stories that go with them. You can use the coloring pages from each week as a timeline and to aid in reviewing.

OPTIONAL EXTRA ACTIVITIES

BUNCHES OF GRAPES

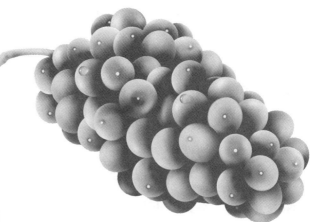

WHAT YOU NEED

- Purple paint
- Small paper plates
- Paper-towel tubes, one for each child
- White construction paper
- Green crayons or markers

Optional

- Smocks or paint shirts, one for each child

WHAT YOU SAY

In our story, God's people found some wonderful things inside the Promised Land. One thing they found were huge bunches of grapes. In fact, the Bible tells us that the grapes were so big, two people had to carry them on a pole in between them. Let's make some big grapes today!

WHAT YOU PREPARE

Pour a small amount of purple paint onto a paper plate. Prepare one plate for each child.

WHAT YOU DO

OPTIONAL: Children put on smocks or paint shirts.

1. Give each child a paper-towel tube. Children dip it into the paint and then press onto the white construction paper in order to make a purple circle.

2. Children make additional circles, clustering them to make a bunch of grapes.

3. When done making grapes, children use green crayons or markers to add a stem.

4. Pick one child's paper and count the number of grapes together as a group.

TEACHING TIP: Print each child's name on their paper along with the Bible reference for the story.

PRESCHOOL SKILLS

- Exploring art materials
- Counting
- Identifying a circle

Optional

- Putting on a smock or shirt

WHAT WERE THEY FEELING?

WHAT YOU NEED

- Emotion Faces, page 31
- Scissors or paper cutter
- Tape or glue
- Craft sticks
- Fine-tip marker or pen

Optional

- Laminator

WHAT YOU PREPARE

Copy and cut out the Emotion Faces. Glue or tape each face to a craft stick.

OPTIONAL: Laminate sheet before cutting out the faces.

WHAT YOU DO

1. Read the Bible story from page 00 or a children's Bible. Pause at various points in the story, and ask children to point to the face that shows what the people in the story might be feeling.

2. As time and interest allow, continue play by holding up the faces one by one and asking the children when people might feel that particular emotion.

PRESCHOOL SKILLS

- Identifying emotions

HIDE THE SPIES

WHAT YOU NEED

- 12 toy men

WHAT YOU PREPARE

Before class, hide the toy people in the room.

PRESCHOOL SKILLS

- Counting
- Increasing attention span

WHAT YOU SAY

When God's people arrived at the Promised Land, twelve men went into the land to spy it out. They were trying to figure out what the land was like without anyone seeing them. Guess what! There are twelve spies hidden in our room just like there were at the Promised Land. Let's find them!

WHAT YOU DO

1. Children search for the toy people.

2. As each is found, count until all twelve men are found. Then, count all of the spies again as a group.

SPY BINOCULARS

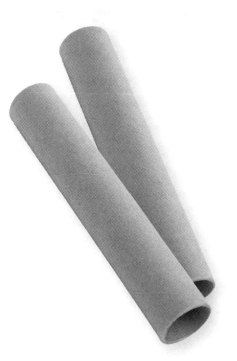

WHAT YOU NEED

- Paper-towel or toilet-paper tubes, two per child
- Crayons or markers
- Stapler

Optional

- Binoculars

WHAT YOU DO

1. Give each child two small cardboard tubes. Children decorate tubes with crayons or markers.

2. When children are done decorating tubes, staple them together in the middle.

ALTERNATE IDEAS: Children use stickers to decorate binoculars. Staple a length of yarn to each pair of binoculars to use as a carrying strap.

OPTIONAL: Children take turns looking through the binoculars.

WHAT YOU SAY

In our Bible account today, men went into the Promised Land to see what it was like. They did not have anything like binoculars. How do you think things would have been different if they'd had REAL binoculars?

PRESCHOOL SKILLS

- Fine-motor skills

C is for Caleb.

Caleb trusted God.

Instant Bible Lessons for Preschoolers: A to Z Thru the Bible

C is for Caleb.

The other ten spies did not understand.
Caleb was right and the other
guys were wrong.

EMOTION FACES

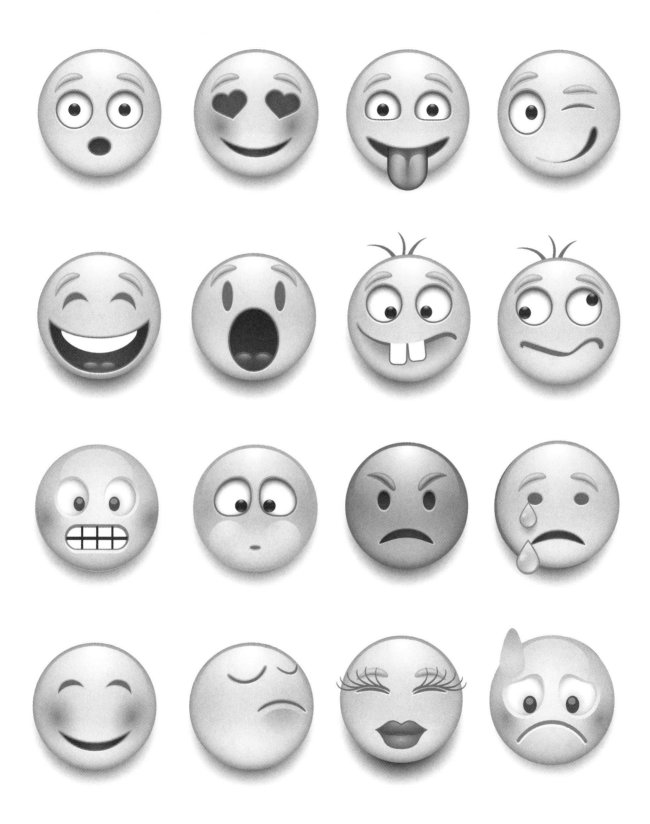

D Is for Dancing

Exodus 14—15

INTRODUCTION

When I am excited or happy, I just can't help but do a little dancing. Turns out, many people in the Bible were the same way! We see many instances of people celebrating and praising God by dancing. In this lesson, we're going to look specifically at Miriam, the sister of Moses. In Exodus 14, we see the Israelites (God's chosen people) at a very scary moment. The armies of Egypt are chasing after them and they are standing face to face with a giant sea with no plan of escape. God told Moses to stretch out his hand over the sea and when Moses obeyed, the sea split in two so the Israelites could safely escape (Exodus 14:15–18). Miriam was so happy when she reached the other side that she burst into singing and dancing, praising God for all that he had done.

OPENING ACTIVITY

FREEZE DANCE

WHAT YOU NEED

- Children's worship music and player

WHAT YOU DO

1. Children spread out in the room so that they are not touching each other.
2. Play the music as children wiggle and dance.
3. When you stop the music, children freeze. They stay frozen until you begin music again.
4. Continue play as time and interest allow.

WHAT YOU SAY

In our true story today, God did something amazing for his people. He sent wind that was SO STRONG, it blew a path right through a giant sea of water! God's people, the Israelites, were able to cross through the sea on dry land. The people were so happy that God helped them! They praised God with singing and dancing.

THE BIBLE STORY

Exodus 14—15

Long ago, God's people were trapped in a land called Egypt. They were slaves and they had to work very hard for the Egyptians.

The people were sad and prayed that God would help them. God sent Moses to save the people and take them out of the land.

As the people were leaving Egypt, the Egyptian king, Pharaoh, and his armies chased after them. It looked like God's people would be captured again. But God had a plan!

God sent a strong wind and divided the sea so that his people could cross on dry land. God saved them!

When the Israelites reached the other side, they were so happy. Moses and his sister Miriam began to sing a song of praise to the Lord. They told about God's mighty works and all the ways that God had rescued them.

Miriam took a tambourine and began to dance with it. The other women followed Miriam, and together, they all danced as a way of praising the Lord.

I WONDER . . .

After the story, read these "wonder" statements and questions out loud to your group. Encourage children to respond.

- I wonder how God's people felt as they walked through the sea. What do you think the people felt about being saved by God?
- I wonder what kinds of things the people saw as they walked through the waters. What things might you see if you could look into a sea?
- I wonder how Miriam felt as she began to sing and dance for the Lord. How does singing and dancing make you feel?
- What do you wonder about our Bible story?

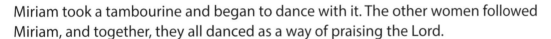

ALPHABET REVIEW

Take a few minutes to go over the letters you have recently learned and the Bible stories that go with them. You can use the coloring pages from each week as a timeline and to aid in reviewing.

OPTIONAL EXTRA ACTIVITIES

TAMBOURINES

WHAT YOU NEED

- Sturdy paper plates, one for each child
- Beans or jingle bells
- Stapler

Optional

- Children's worship music and player

WHAT YOU DO

1. Children color the backs of their paper plates (on the back).

2. Assist children in folding paper plates in half. Staple plate closed, leaving a small opening.

3. Children fill their paper-plate with beans or jingle bells. Adults staple tambourines closed.

OPTIONAL: Play music so that children can dance and sing with their new tambourines.

PRESCHOOL SKILLS

- **Fine-motor skills**
- **Hearing and appeciating music**

I CAN PRAISE GOD FOR . . .

WHAT YOU NEED

- Praise Paper, page 38
- Crayons or markers

WHAT YOU PREPARE

For each child, make a copy of Praise Paper.

WHAT YOU DO

1. Children print their names in the blank on the page. Print names for children as needed.

2. In the space provided, children draw a picture of what they are thankful for.

PRESCHOOL SKILLS

- **Printing name**
- **Drawing**

WHAT YOU SAY

What are some things you are thankful for? What would you like to praise God for today? Let's draw what we're thankful for on our papers.

RUN FROM THE EGYPTIANS

WHAT YOU NEED

● Large play area

WHAT YOU DO

1. Children play a game like Sharks and Minnows. Children stand against one wall.

2. Select one or two volunteers to stand in the middle of the room and serve as "Egyptians."

3. On your signal, children run from one side of the room to the other, avoiding the Egyptians as best they can.

4. If they are tagged by an Egyptian, they sit down on the side.

5. After a few moments, choose new volunteer(s) to be the Egyptians and play again as time and interest allow.

PRESCHOOL SKILLS

● Gross-motor skills

TEACHING TIP: When a child is "out," don't make them remain out if they want to play. It's hard for little ones to sit still, and the purpose of the game is to have fun—not to find a winner.

WHAT YOU SAY

In this game, it was pretty hard to avoid those Egyptians. It was the same for the Israelites a long time ago. Thankfully, God provided a pretty amazing way for his people to escape the Egyptians.

SAND AND WATER

PRESCHOOL SKILLS

● Fine-motor skills
● Story recall

WHAT YOU NEED

● Sand
● Blue fish-tank pebbles (available at discount and pet stores)
● Large, shallow container (cardboard box, baking pan, etc.)
● Toy people

WHAT YOU PREPARE

Pour the sand into the shallow container. In the middle of the container, place the pebbles to represent the Red Sea. Place the toy people on one side of the "sea."

WHAT YOU DO

1. Children work together to "split" the sea by moving the pebbles to the side and helping the toy people walk through to the other side.

2. Children play freely after reenacting the story.

D d

D D D D

d d d d

D is for dancing.

Miriam danced
for God.

D is for dancing.

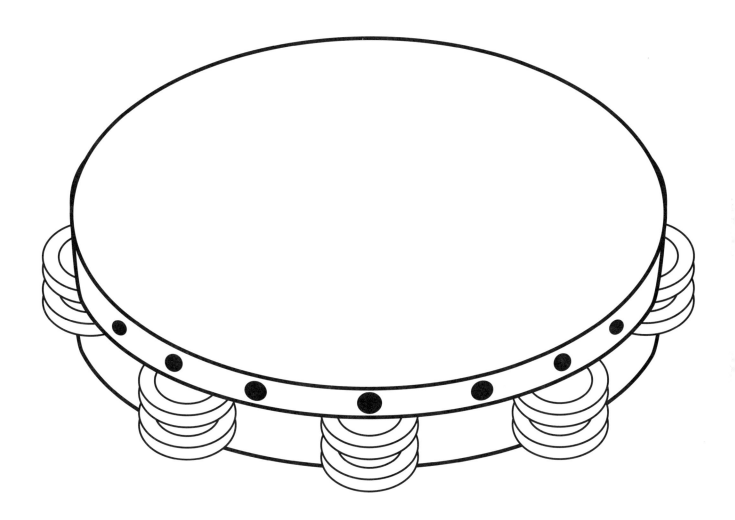

God helped the Israelites cross the sea.
They were so happy, they had a jamboree.
Miriam danced to praise God's name.
The women joined in and danced the same.

● ● ● ● ● ● ●
PRAISE PAPER

In the space, draw a picture of what you praise God for.

_____ can praise God with dancing

and singing. We praise God for _____.

E Is for Elijah

1 Kings 18

INTRODUCTION

Elijah the prophet had a very shaky relationship with the king of Israel, King Ahab, and an even more dangerous relationship with Jezebel, the queen. Queen Jezebel was a woman bent on evil and she spent several years finding God's prophets and putting them to death. Because the leaders of God's people had fallen so far away from worshiping the one true God, the Lord had sent a terrible famine in the land. For three years, no rain had fallen and the people were running out of food, both for themselves and their animals. One day, Elijah was sent by the Lord to show them who the one true God was—and it was done in an amazing way!

OPENING ACTIVITY

ROCK STACKING

WHAT YOU NEED

- Flat rocks

WHAT YOU DO

1. Children play with and stack the rocks.
2. Children try to make a rock tower as tall as they can.
3. After a few minutes, take some of the rocks and build an altar with them.

What You Say

In our true story today, a man named Elijah stacked up some rocks. He used bigger rocks to make an altar. An altar is a place where sacrifices are made to worship God. Normally, the people would place the animal on the altar and then set a fire beneath it. In this situation, though, Elijah told the people that God himself would provide the fire—fire from heaven!

THE BIBLE STORY

1 Kings 18

A long time ago, in the land of Israel, there was King named Ahab. King Ahab did not love God and did not follow the commands found in God's Word.

God was not pleased with King Ahab. God sent a man named Elijah to give King Ahab a message. Elijah told King Ahab that he should stop worshiping fake gods. Elijah told King Ahab to start doing right things.

Both the king and the queen were very angry about Elijah's message! They refused to worship the one true God.

Because the king and queen didn't obey, God did not send rain to the land for over three years. The people were very sad. Without rain, they could not grow food for themselves or for their animals.

God sent Elijah to show the people who the one true God is. Elijah invited the prophets who served fake gods to a big mountain. On the mountain, they built two altars—one for the true God and one for a fake god, Baal.

The fake god's prophets prayed and asked for their god to send fire. But nothing happened. They tried all day and nothing happened.

Then it was Elijah's turn. Elijah prayed to the one true Go. Immediately fire WHOOSHED down from heaven! The fire burned up the animal, the sticks, and even the stones! Truly, ours is the one true God!

I WONDER . . .

After the story, read these "wonder" statements and questions out loud to your group. Encourage children to respond.

- I wonder why the king refused to follow the one true God. Why do you think some people don't follow God?

- I wonder why the fake god did not send fire to burn the sacrifice. Why do you think the fake god couldn't send fire?

- I wonder what it would have been like to see fire falling from heaven. How do you think you would feel if you were there?

- What do you wonder about our Bible story?

ALPHABET REVIEW

Take a few minutes to go over the letters you have recently learned and the Bible stories that go with them. You can use the coloring pages from each week as a timeline and to aid in reviewing.

OPTIONAL EXTRA ACTIVITIES

UMBRELLA TIME

WHAT YOU NEED

- Thunderstorm or rain sounds and player
- Umbrellas and/or lengths of fabric

WHAT YOU SAY

After the fire fell from heaven, the people knew who the one true God was. They worshiped him and God sent rain to the land. In this game, we are going to put up our umbrellas (or fabric) whenever we hear the sound of rain and then put them down again then the rain stops.

WHAT YOU DO

1. Give each child an umbrella or length of fabric. Children walk about the room listening for the sound of rain.

2. After a few moments, play the thunderstorm or rain sounds.

3. Children open up umbrellas or hold fabric over their heads.

4. After a few moments, pause the sounds. Children close up umbrellas or lower fabric.

5. Continue as time and interest allow.

PRESCHOOL SKILLS

- **Listening skills**
- **Gross-motor skills**

PRAYER REQUESTS

WHAT YOU NEED

- Post-it Notes

WHAT YOU SAY

Just like God heard Elijah's prayers, he hears ours, too. Is there anything you want to pray to God about?

WHAT YOU DO

1. Write down children's prayer requests on Post-it Notes and put them on the wall.

2. Pray aloud for the requests as a group.

PRESCHOOL SKILLS

- **Developing empathy**

SHAPE PICTURE

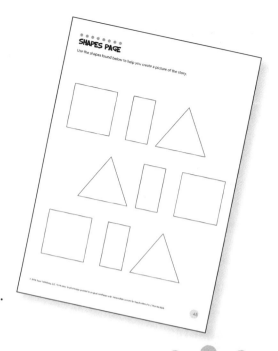

WHAT YOU NEED

- Shapes Page, page 45
- Scissors
- Crayons or markers
- Glue
- Construction paper

WHAT YOU PREPARE

For each child, make at least one copy of Shapes Page.

WHAT YOU DO

1. Children use crayons or markers to color shapes and then cut out shapes with their scissors.

2. Children make a picture to go with the Bible story, by gluing the shapes to construction paper.

3. Children add more details with crayons or markers.

TEACHING TIP: Name the different shapes children are using. Children identify and say the names of the shapes with you.

PRESCHOOL SKILLS

- Scissor skills
- Identifying basic shapes
- Cutting basic shapes

RAINSTORM

WHAT YOU SAY

In our story, it did not rain for three years. After God sent fire from heaven and the people turned from doing bad things, God sent rain to the land. It started as a very small cloud in the distance, but soon the sky grew black with clouds and the rain was came down harder and harder!

WHAT YOU DO

1. Instruct children to carefully copy the following movements:
   - Rub your hands together to make a sound like wind.
   - Tap one finger on the other palm hand to represent the first raindrops.
   - Tap all four fingers on opposite palm for many more rain drops.
   - After a few moments, clap rapidly to make the sound of more intense rain.
   - Loudly slap the floor to make thunder!

2. Vary motions and Increase the intensity for a few moments. Then reduce the noise level as the "storm" dies down.

PRESCHOOL SKILLS

- Gross-motor skills
- Following directions
- Identifying body parts

E is for Elijah.

Elijah worshiped God.

E is for Elijah.

Elijah stood on a mountain top.
Worship of fake gods had to stop!
Elijah prayed to heaven and fire fell down.
The people worshiped God,
all through the town.

Use the shapes found below to help you create a picture of the story.

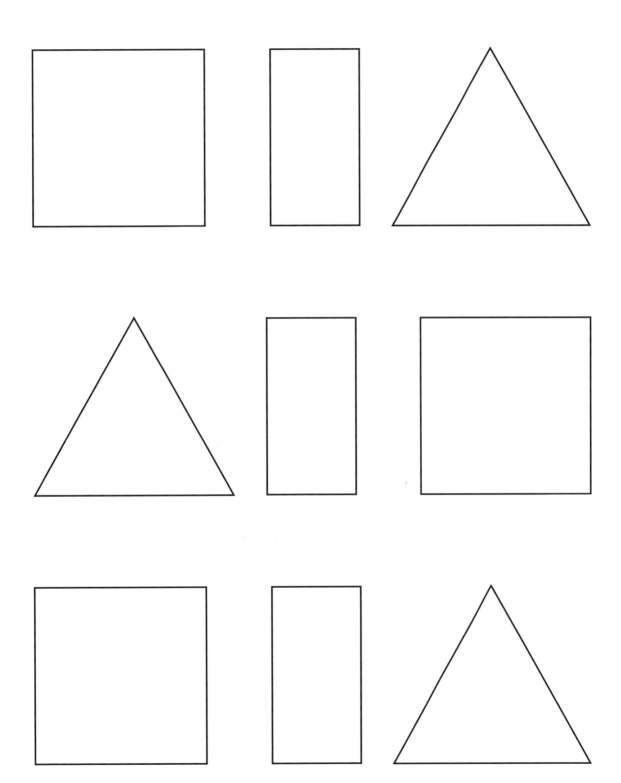

F Is for Fish

Jonah 1–2

• • • • • • • •
INTRODUCTION

Mercy is something that we love to get, but don't often love to give. Such was the case with a man named Jonah. Jonah was given a mission by God to travel to a land called Nineveh. Nineveh was famous for being a land of sin and Jonah did not think they deserved mercy. So instead of obeying, God, Jonah came up with his own plan. However, when things didn't go the way Jonah had hoped, he was looking for some mercy for himself—for disobeying God!

OPENING ACTIVITY

• • • • • • • •
COLORFUL FISH

WHAT YOU NEED

● Colorful plastic fish, at least ten

WHAT YOU SAY

In our true story today, a man named Jonah was out on a boat when a rather amazing thing happened! I won't tell you the whole story, but it has something to do with a fish. I brought a few fish for us to look at today. Can you tell me what colors these fish are? (Children respond.)

WHAT YOU DO

1. Children explore the different colors on the fish, grouping them by color, setting them in different patterns (red, green, blue, red, green, blue, etc.), or counting the total fish in each color.

2. After done exploring colors, children count the total number of fish.

ALTERNATE IDEA: Instead of using plastic fish, use the Fish Template on page 00 to cut colorful fish from sheets of construction paper.

THE BIBLE STORY

Jonah 1–2

Many years ago, there was a city called Nineveh. Nineveh was full of people who did not love God and did not follow his commandments. God was very upset about this. He did not want people to continue to live in their sin, so he decided to send a messenger to this land.

The messenger's name was Jonah. God told Jonah to travel to Nineveh and warn the people. God wanted the people to turn away from their sins and start living God's way.

Jonah was not happy about this! Instead of obeying God, he set sail for a land called Tarshish.

When he was on the boat, a great storm arose. It was clear that God was unhappy with Jonah. Jonah told the sailors on the boat to throw him into the sea. The sailors did! Jonah was thrown into the sea and the waves grew calm.

God provided a fish to swallow Jonah. While inside the fish (for three days and nights!), Jonah realized he was wrong. He prayed and asked God to forgive him. God did indeed forgive Jonah. God told the fish to spit Jonah out and the fish obeyed. After this amazing event, Jonah obeyed God.

I WONDER . . .

After the story, read these "wonder" statements and questions out loud to your group. Encourage children to respond.

- I wonder why Jonah did not want to go to Nineveh. Why do you think Jonah didn't want to go there?
- I wonder what the sailors were thinking when a giant storm started. How do you think you would have felt?
- I wonder if the people Nineveh had ever heard about God before Jonah came. Do you think they might have acted differently if they had?
- What else do you wonder about Jonah and the giant fish?

ALPHABET REVIEW

Take a few minutes to go over the letters you have recently learned and the Bible stories that go with them. You can use the coloring pages from each week as a timeline and to aid in reviewing.

OPTIONAL EXTRA ACTIVITIES

FOLLOW THE LEADER

WHAT YOU DO

1. Begin the game as the leader.

2. Children follow after you, copying your actions as you walk: stomping your feet, hopping, skipping, hopping on one foot, crawling, etc.

3. After a few moments, select another child to be the leader. Continue as time and interest allow.

WHAT YOU SAY

In this game, you guys did an amazing job following the leader. You really listened (or watched!) and obeyed. In our true story today, Jonah did not obey. In fact, he did almost the exact opposite of what God told him to do. Life always turns out best when we listen and obey.

> **PRESCHOOL SKILLS**
>
> - **Listening skills**
> - **Gross-motor skills: hopping, running, skipping, etc.**

PLAY DOUGH FISH

WHAT YOU NEED

- Play dough
- Fish-shaped cookie cutters

Optional

- Play dough tools
- Small gems

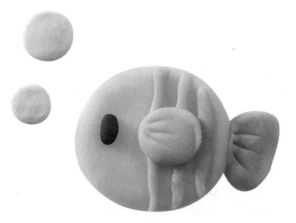

WHAT YOU DO

1. Give each child a fist-sized lump of play dough and a cookie cutter.

2. Children make fish with their play dough. While children work, discuss the colors they are using.

OPTIONAL: Children add designs on their fish with the tools or gems.

ALTERNATE IDEA: Use salt dough. Children paint the fish when they are dry.

> **PRESCHOOL SKILLS**
>
> - **Fine-motor skills**
> - **Identify colors**

PAPER PLATE FISH

WHAT YOU NEED

- Paper plates
- Scissors
- Stapler
- Crayons or markers

Optional

- Smocks or paint shirts, one for each child

PRESCHOOL SKILLS

- **Scissor skills**
- **Color recognition**

Optional

- **Putting on a smock or shirt**

WHAT YOU DO

OPTIONAL: Children put on smocks or paint shirts.

1. Children cut a small triangle out of the front of the plate. The opening will be the fish's mouth.
2. Staple the triangle to the back of the plate to serve as the tail.
3. Children use markers to draw an eye on the fish and to color the fish. Discuss the colors children use.

NAME OF ACTIVITY

WHAT YOU NEED

- Fish Template, page 52
- Crayons or markers
- Scissors
- Glue
- Blue construction paper

WHAT YOU PREPARE

For each child, make a copy of the Fish Template. Make a few extra for children with more than six letters in their name.

PRESCHOOL SKILLS

- **Scissor skills**
- **Recognizing first name in print**
- **Naming letters**

WHAT YOU DO

1. Give each child a copy of the Fish Template.
2. Children color the fish and then cut them out with scissors.
3. Using a crayon or marker, to print the letters of each child's name on that child's fish, one letter per fish.
4. Help children glue the fish in order onto the construction paper.

ENRICHMENT IDEA: As children work, sing "Jonah's Song" on page 8.

F is for fish.

The fish swallowed Jonah.

F is for fish.

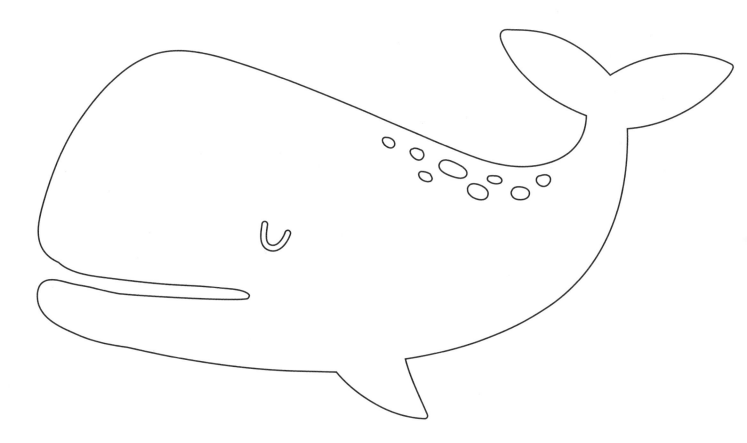

Jonah heard a command from God.
But Jonah thought God's plan was flawed.
Instead of listening, he ran away.
Got swallowed by a fish, then
promised to obey.

FISH TEMPLATE

G Is for Goliath

1 Samuel 17

INTRODUCTION

Goliath was a Philistine, an enemy to God's people. When the Israelites (God's people) and the Philistines were engaged in battle, Goliath would come out every morning and every evening and taunt the Israelites. He asked for a man to fight, but all the Israelites ran in fear (1 Samuel 17:24). David, a young shepherd had come to the battle grounds to bring food to his brothers. When David heard what Goliath was saying, he was shocked. He knew the way Goliath was talking about the one true God was wrong and David decided to do something about it. Goliath trusted in his size, strength, and armor to win the battle. David trusted in the Lord God.

OPENING ACTIVITY

BIG AND TALL

WHAT YOU NEED

- Tape measure

WHAT YOU DO

1. Take children to a place on your church campus where there are tall pieces of furniture or tall structures (perhaps a playground).

2. Work together to measure the objects around you.

What You Say

In our true story today, a man named Goliath wanted to fight against God's people. Goliath was a giant—taller than almost anyone you've probably ever seen. He stood about 9 feet and 9 inches tall—which is almost 10 feet tall. An elephant is anywhere from 8 to 13 feet tall—so Goliath might have been taller than an elephant. Can you imagine that? Most school buses are about 10.5 feet tall—so Goliath would almost be as tall as one. That's hard to believe!

THE BIBLE STORY

1 Samuel 17

Long ago, God's people were fighting against a people group called the Philistines. The Philistines did not love the one true God and would often tease the Israelites.

There was one man, Goliath, who was a champion fighter. Goliath was very tall and very strong. Goliath thought that nothing could stop him. He trusted in his own strength and power to win his battles.

However, God is more powerful than anything or anyone! God had a plan to defeat Goliath and bring victory to his people, the Israelites.

A young man named David came to the battle grounds to give his brothers food. David was a shepherd, which means that he spent his days watching the family sheep and keeping them from harm. In the past, David had to fight off a lion and a bear to keep his sheep safe. David knew that God protected him when he had to fight off wild beasts and he trusted that God would do the same thing if he fought Goliath.

The king was happy that someone wanted to go against Goliath and he tried to give David armor to wear. However, David trusted in the Lord. He did not need the armor. David took five stones and his slingshot. With God's help, David defeated Goliath by hitting him right in the head with a stone!

Even though Goliath was big and strong, David won because of God's power.

I WONDER . . .

After the story, read these "wonder" statements and questions out loud to your group. Encourage children to respond.

- I wonder why no one else was willing to fight Goliath. Do you think you would have wanted to fight Goliath? Why or why not?

- I wonder why David was not afraid of the giant. Why do you think David was so brave?

- I wonder what Goliath thought when he first saw David coming to battle him. What do you think Goliath said when he saw David?

- What do you wonder about our Bible story?

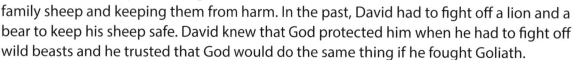

ALPHABET REVIEW

Take a few minutes to go over the letters you have recently learned and the Bible stories that go with them. You can use the coloring pages from each week as a timeline and to aid in reviewing.

OPTIONAL EXTRA ACTIVITIES

SMOOTH STONES

WHAT YOU NEED

- Flat, smooth stones, at least one per child
- Paint or markers

Optional

- Smocks or paint shirts, one for each child

WHAT YOU DO

OPTIONAL: Children put on smocks or paint shirts.

1. Children each select a stone and color on it.
2. Children carry their rock as a reminder that God is with them.

WHAT YOU SAY

David fought a giant even though he only had a few stones. He was brave because he knew that God was with him.

THE BATTLE IS THE LORD'S

WHAT YOU NEED

- Rocking Words, page 60
- Scissors
- Glue
- Construction paper

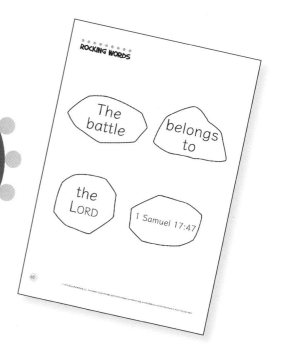

WHAT YOU PREPARE

For each child, make a copy of Rocking Words.

WHAT YOU DO

1. Children color the rocks and then cut them out.
2. Children glue the rocks onto a piece of construction paper and then decorate the rest of the page. For example, they can draw water so that the rocks are in a stream).

TARGET PRACTICE

WHAT YOU NEED

- Construction paper
- Masking tape
- Ping-Pong balls

WHAT YOU PREPARE

Cut sheet of construction paper into a circle shape to make a target. Tape the target on the wall above the heads of the children.

WHAT YOU DO

1. Give a child five Ping-Pong balls. Child tosses balls to try to hit the circle.

2. Repeat until each child has at least one turn. Repeat as time and interest allow.

WHAT YOU SAY

It's not always easy to hit our target, is it? When David was on that battle field, he only had one chance to really defeat Goliath. By God's power though, David hit right on the mark!

PRESCHOOL SKILLS

- **Throwing skills**
- **Gross-motor skills**

PAPER-PLATE PEOPLE

WHAT YOU NEED

- Paper plates (not Styrofoam), one for each child
- Markers
- Craft sticks
- Packing tape

Optional

- Yarn
- Glue

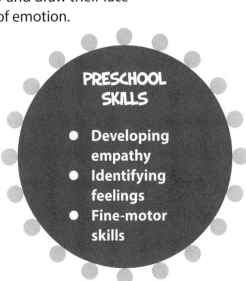

WHAT YOU SAY

Talk with children about how everyone must have been feeling on the battle field. **How did Goliath feel? How did the Israelite army feel? How did the king feel? How did David feel?**

WHAT YOU DO

1. Children pick out one of the people from the Bible story and draw their face onto the paper plate. Encourage children to draw a lot of emotion.

2. When finished drawing, help children tape a craft stick to the back of the paper plate.

3. If time allows, reenact the story with the children using their paper-plate people.

OPTIONAL: Children cut small pieces of yarn for hair and glue them to the paper-plate people.

PRESCHOOL SKILLS

- **Developing empathy**
- **Identifying feelings**
- **Fine-motor skills**

G g

G G G G

g g g g

G is for Goliath.

Goliath was defeated.

G is for Goliath.

Goliath was a giant, standing
nearly ten feet tall.
But Goliath did not worship
the one true God at all.
David came to fight with only one small stone
God helped him hit that giant,
who fell down with a groan.

The
battle

belongs
to

the
LORD.

1 Samuel 17:47

H Is for Hannah

1 Samuel 1–2

INTRODUCTION

Hannah was a woman who loved the Lord. Every year, when she went to the temple to worship, she would ask God for a child, but the Lord had not granted her request. Even still, Hannah did not give up and did not turn her back on the Lord. She persevered in her prayer. It wasn't always easy. Many times, Peninnah (another wife) would tease her and make Hannah so upset that she could not eat. Finally, one year, Eli the priest saw Hannah praying. He encouraged her and prayed that the Lord would grant her request. Not long after, Hannah became pregnant. God answered her prayer!

OPENING ACTIVITY

CHEER HER UP

WHAT YOU DO

1. Begin by pretending that you are sad. Ask the children to help cheer you up.

2. After a few minutes, begin smile and thank the children for their help.

3. Other children volunteer to pretend to be sad while others bring good cheer.

WHAT YOU SAY

In our true story today, a woman named Hannah was very sad. She wanted a baby, but it did not seem like the Lord was going to give her a child. Another woman named Peninnah saw how upset Hannah was. Instead of cheering her up, Peninnah made things worse! She would tease Hannah and say mean things to her. I'm so glad that's not how we're acting. I like cheering someone up much more than making them upset.

THE BIBLE STORY

1 Samuel 1–2

Have you ever really REALLY wanted something? Wanted it so bad that you think about it when you wake up and you might even dream about when you go to sleep. Once, there was a woman named Hannah who felt the same way!

Hannah really wanted a baby. Every year, she would go to the temple to worship the one true God. When she was there, she would pray and ask God for a baby. But year after year, it didn't happen. Can you imagine how that felt?

Hannah became more upset and more disappointed as time went on. Her husband tried to cheer her up, but still, she was often sad.

One day, she was praying when a priest named Eli saw her. He encouraged her and prayed that God would give her a baby. Finally, God did indeed give Hannah a baby. She was so delighted.

Then, Hannah did a very strange thing. In order to show God how grateful she was, she allowed her son to live in the temple so that he could serve God. Hannah would bring her son, Samuel, a new robe every year when she came to worship. Samuel grew to love God and Hannah had more children. God is powerful and strong and he does not want us to give up when we pray to him.

I WONDER . . .

After the story, read these "wonder" statements and questions out loud to your group. Encourage children to respond.

- I wonder what Eli thought when he saw Hannah praying. What would you think if you were Eli?
- I wonder how Hannah's husband felt when Hannah could not have a baby. How do you think he felt?
- I wonder why God waited so long to say "yes" to Hannah's prayer. Why do you think God might have waited?
- What do you wonder about our Bible story?

ALPHABET REVIEW

Take a few minutes to go over the letters you have recently learned and the Bible stories that go with them. You can use the coloring pages from each week as a timeline and to aid in reviewing.

OPTIONAL EXTRA ACTIVITIES

PRAYER LETTERS

WHAT YOU NEED

- White paper
- Envelopes
- Crayons or markers

WHAT YOU DO

1. Children decide on something specific to pray about and draw it on their paper.

2. When finished drawing, children put their prayer request inside of the envelope.

3. Help children label the envelope with "To: God" and "From: (child's name)."

OPTIONAL: Write a caption at the bottom of each child's drawing.

PRESCHOOL SKILLS

- Writing name
- Fine-motor skills

WHAT YOU SAY

Now that our prayer requests are in envelopes, where should we send them? (Children respond.) **We don't need to mail them, do we? We can pray out loud and God hears us—isn't that amazing? I'm so glad that God hears all our prayers.**

HAPPY AND SAD

WHAT YOU NEED

Optional

- Children's Bible

WHAT YOU DO

1. Re-read Hannah's story from this book or from a children's Bible.

2. Stop at key points in the story and ask the children how the people might be feeling.

3. Children make happy faces or sad faces to match the feelings in the story.

PRESCHOOL SKILLS

- Developing empathy
- Identifying feelings

RHYME TIME

WHAT YOU SAY

There were lots of things we read about in today's story. Right now, we are going to play a game with the things we learned about. I will say a word and you will try to say something that rhymes. It's okay if it's just a nonsense word!

WORDS FOR GAME

Pray, go, walk, baby, child, coat, robe, love, sad, happy, mean, nice, tease, help, etc.

PRESCHOOL SKILLS

- Identifies rhyming words

WHERE IS BABY?

WHAT YOU NEED

- Hannah Maze, page 67
- Crayons or markers

WHAT YOU SAY

For each child, make a copy of Hannah Maze.

WHAT YOU DO

1. Children follow the dotted line with their finger in order to find the baby.
2. Then, children trace the dotted line with a crayon or marker.

PRESCHOOL SKILLS

- Following directions
- Pre-writing skills

H is for Hannah.

Hannah prayed to God.

H is for Hannah.

Hannah prayed for a child for many years.
She knelt at the temple and cried many tears.
God heard Hannah pray and gave her a son.
Hannah praised God for all he had done.

HANNAH MAZE

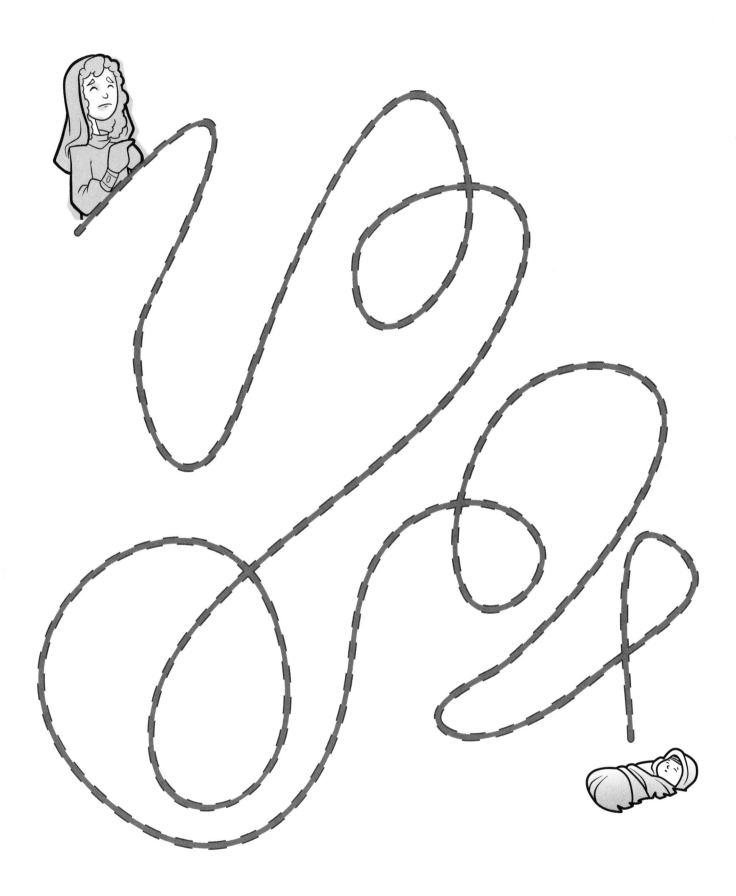

I Is for Innkeeper

Luke 2

INTRODUCTION

God's people had been promised a Savior, someone who would rescue them from their sins. No one would have guessed that this great and mighty Messiah would come in such a humble way. God had chosen Mary and Joseph to be Jesus' earthly parents. This couple had to take a long journey to Bethlehem. When they arrived, there was no room for them in the inn. Imagine how exhausted and discouraged they must have been. One inn keeper allowed them to stay in a stable. It wasn't much, but it was where the King of kings would be born. Later, Jesus' birth would be proclaimed by angels and the place of his birth would be marked by a special star.

OPENING ACTIVITY

NO ROOM

WHAT YOU NEED

- Chairs, one fewer than the number of children
- Children's worship music and player

WHAT YOU PREPARE

Set up chairs in a circle, facing inward.

WHAT YOU DO

1. Children play a game of musical chairs, walking around the circle as you play music.

2. After a few moments, stop the music. Children all try to sit down.
   Child who can't find a chair sits off to the side.

3. Eliminate one chair and play again. Continue, eliminating a chair at every round.

4. After a few rounds, take away all the chairs. When children say there's no place for them to sit, use "What You Say" conversation.

WHAT YOU SAY

In our true story today, there was a couple who traveled a long way. They were looking for a place to stay, but just like in our game, there wasn't enough room for everyone. They got pushed out and didn't have anywhere to rest. Did any of you run out of room to sit? How did it feel? (Children respond.) **Mary can Joseph probably felt many of those things, too. But God provided a place for them, even though it wasn't what they were expecting!**

THE BIBLE STORY

Luke 2

God had promised to send someone special into the world—someone who would save people from the punishment for their sins. This special person was God's Son, Jesus.

Jesus came to Earth in a very unusual way for the King of kings. Instead of coming down through the clouds, Jesus was born as a baby. God chose a couple named Mary and Joseph to raise the baby Jesus. Mary was pregnant when she and Joseph had to take a big trip to Bethlehem. It must have been hard to travel that far! When they arrived, it was almost time for Mary to have the baby, but there was some bad news.

Mary and Joseph looked and looked, but they could not find an inn to stay in. There was no room for them. A kind innkeeper showed them a stable or cave to stay inside instead. Jesus was born and placed in a manger instead of a crib. A manger is usually where the food for the animals is put. What a strange place to put a baby!

This is probably not what Mary and Joseph were expecting, but it was all part of God's perfect plan for his son, Jesus.

I WONDER . . .

After the story, read these "wonder" statements and questions out loud to your group. Encourage children to respond.

- I wonder what the place where Jesus was born was like. What do you think it looked like? What do you think it smelled like?

- I wonder how Mary and Joseph felt when Jesus was born. What are some of the feelings they must have had?

- I wonder how God felt when his Son, Jesus, was born. How do you feel knowing that Jesus was born?

- What do you wonder about our Bible story?

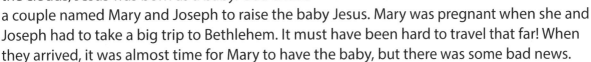

ALPHABET REVIEW

Take a few minutes to go over the letters you have recently learned and the Bible stories that go with them. You can use the coloring pages from each week as a timeline and to aid in reviewing.

OPTIONAL EXTRA ACTIVITIES

WHO IS IT?

WHAT YOU DO

1. Children stand near a door. Select one volunteer to be the innkeeper.

2. Innkeeper stands apart from the group and turns away from the children. If child is willing, ask them to close their eyes.

3. Choose another child to go outside the room with an adult helper and knock on the door.

4. The innkeeper opens up the door a little, but doesn't look at the child outside. Innkeeper asks "Who Is It?"

5. The child who knocked answers "It is me!"

6. The innkeeper tries to guess who knocked on the door. Give the innkeeper three guesses..

7. Whether or not the innkeeper ever guesses correctly, the child who knocked then becomes the innkeeper and play continues until everyone has a chance to be the innkeeper or as time and interest allow.

PRESCHOOL SKILLS

- Using the hearing sense

OPEN AND SHUT

WHAT YOU NEED

- At the Inn, page 74
- Scissors
- Glue
- Crayons or markers
- Construction paper

WHAT YOU PREPARE

For each child, make a copy of At the Inn.

WHAT YOU DO

1. Children cut out the inn and around the people.

2. Children cut on the dotted lines on the door so that it can open.

3. Children glue the inn on a piece of construction paper, being careful not to glue the door shut.

4. Children glue the innkeeper inside the door and then glue Mary and Joseph on a part of the paper away from the inn.

5. Children use their paper inn and characters to retell the Bible story.

HOW CAN WE HELP?

WHAT YOU SAY

Mary and Joseph probably could have used a little help when it came time for the baby to be born. There are people all around us that might need a little help, too. Let's talk about the following situations and think of ways we can help others.

WHAT YOU DO

1. Read the following scenarios and brainstorm as a group ways to help others.

   - The back-door area is a mess where everyone comes in and takes off their shoes.
   - Your bedroom floor is messy with dirty clothes.
   - The kitchen table is dirty.
   - Mom is very thirsty, but is holding the baby.
   - The kitchen floor has dirt on it.
   - The plants at your house are in need of some water.
   - Your next-door neighbor is elderly and doesn't have many visitors.
   - There is a child at the playground with no one else to play with.
   - Sometimes you see people who are hungry and have no home.
   - Someone at your church is feeling sick.
   - The animals at the local shelter don't get much attention.

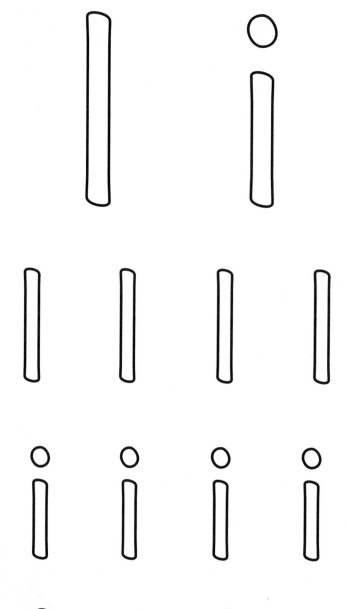

I is for innkeeper.

The innkeeper helped.

I is for innkeeper.

The innkeeper was busy and
he was out of space.
For Mary and Joseph, he
did not have a place.
He took them to the stable
where they could be warm.
And this is where baby Jesus would be born.

AT THE INN

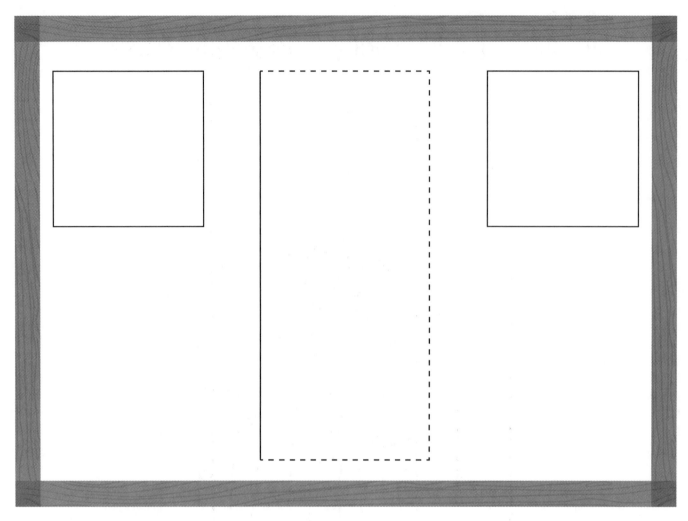

J Is for Joseph

Genesis 37, 39, 41, 45

INTRODUCTION

A man named Jacob had many sons. There was one son, though, that he loved more than any of the others. Jacob loved his son Joseph the best and made him a special robe with many colors to show his love. As you can imagine, this special treatment did not sit well with the other brothers. Soon they were so jealous and angry with Joseph that they threw him into a pit. Their bad behavior did not end there. When a group of merchants passed by, the brothers pulled Joseph out of the pit, and sold him to the merchants who were headed to Egypt. This may seem like the end of the story, but God had a different plan!

OPENING ACTIVITY

TAKE MY ROBE TAG

WHAT YOU NEED

- Colorful blanket

WHAT YOU SAY

Place a colorful blanket across your shoulders. **Pretend that I am Joseph and this blanket is my colorful robe. The rest of you are the angry brothers, trying to take the robe away! When I move, try to tag me!**

WHAT YOU DO

1. Children try to tag "Joseph."
2. Once Joseph is tagged, the robe is given to the tagger.
3. Tagger puts on blanket to become Joseph and play continues as time and interest allow.

THE BIBLE STORY

Genesis 37, 39, 41, 45

Long ago, a man named Jacob had many children. Though Jacob loved all of his children, there was one son for whom he did something very special. Jacob gave his son Joseph a beautiful coat with many colors. This was a real honor and Joseph's brothers were mad!

In fact, the brothers were so mad that they decided to get rid of Joseph. When they saw some merchants in the desert headed to Egypt one day, they took Joseph and sold him away. The brothers were being mean, but God would use this situation for good.

Joseph lived in Egypt for a time with a man named Potiphar. He helped Potiphar and took good care of his home. One day, Joseph was accused of doing something wrong. Even though Joseph did nothing wrong, he was put in jail. Joseph must have felt sad and confused, but he continued to help others.

When Pharaoh, the king, needed help interpreting a dream, he sent for Joseph. Joseph helped Pharaoh and was given a new job. Joseph was now in command over all of Egypt! Joseph helped the people gather food and store it so they would be ready for an upcoming famine. A famine means there is very little food. Even the nearby countries were suffering since there was almost no food.

One day, Joseph's brothers came to Egypt to buy food. Joseph was surprised! He decided to forgive his brothers and help them even though they had been mean to him so many years ago.

I WONDER . . .

After the story, read these "wonder" statements and questions out loud to your group. Encourage children to respond.

- I wonder if Joseph's brothers felt bad about selling Joseph. How would you have felt if you were one of Joseph's brothers?

- I wonder why Joseph kept helping people even though so many bad things happened. Why do you think Joseph wanted to help others?

- I wonder how Joseph felt when he saw his brothers come to buy food. What do you think he said to his brothers?

- What do you wonder about our Bible story?

ALPHABET REVIEW

Take a few minutes to go over the letters you have recently learned and the Bible stories that go with them. You can use the coloring pages from each week as a timeline and to aid in reviewing.

OPTIONAL EXTRA ACTIVITIES

CUP OF FOOD

WHAT YOU NEED

- Large bowl
- Snack food (dry cereal, crackers, etc.)
- Spoon
- Small paper or plastic bowls, one per child

WHAT YOU PREPARE

Fill the large bowl with the snack food.

WHAT YOU SAY

Give each child a small bowl. **People came from far and wide to buy food from Egypt. Their food bowls were empty, like your bowls are empty. Because Joseph had prepared for the famine, he had food saved. His bowl of food was full, like this large bowl is full. Let's pretend that we are the people who needed food from Joseph during the famine.**

WHAT YOU DO

1. Select one child to be Joseph and stand near the big bowl with the spoon.

2. Children stand in a line. Hand each child a small bowl.

3. Each child approaches Joseph and asks for "a little food."

4. Joseph places a spoonful of food in the cup and says, "God has provided."

5. The last child in the line then becomes Joseph. This time, children ask for "more food."

6. Children take turns being Joseph as time and interest allows.

PRESCHOOL SKILLS

- Pouring
- Understanding concepts: full and empty
- Understanding concepts: a little and more

JOSEPH'S COLORFUL COAT

WHAT YOU NEED

- Joseph's Colorful Coat, page 82
- Colorful strips or scraps of construction paper
- Glue

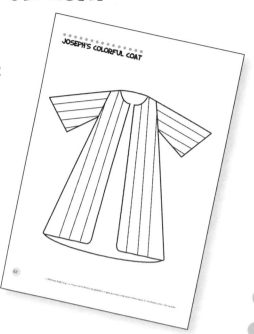

WHAT YOU PREPARE

For each child, make a copy of Joseph's Colorful Coat. Place the strips and scraps of construction paper in the middle of the table where children can reach them.

WHAT YOU DO

1. Children rip the paper into small pieces and then glue them onto the coat paper to make a "colorful coat" for Joseph.

2. When children finish decorating their coats, count how many colors are on each coat.

PRESCHOOL SKILLS

- Fine-motor skills
- Color identification
- Counting

EGYPTIAN DRAMATIC PLAY

WHAT YOU NEED

- Simple robes
- Egyptian costume pieces

Optional

- Snack bowl from Cup of Food activity

WHAT YOU PREPARE

Set up a dramatic play station using costumes and props that are relevant to the Bible story. You can often find Egyptian costumes or simple robes at thrift stores and party stores.

WHAT YOU DO

1. Children dress-up in the robes and costume pieces you provided.

2. Children act out the Bible story.

PRESCHOOL SKILLS

- Pretending
- Remembering and recalling a story
- Self-help skills

COLOR SORT

WHAT YOU NEED

- Colorful strips or scraps of construction paper

WHAT YOU PREPARE

Place the strips and scraps of construction paper in the middle of the table where children can reach them.

WHAT YOU SAY

Joseph's coat had many colors in it. Our world has many colors in it, too. Let's play a color-matching game!

WHAT YOU DO

1. Each child chooses a piece of construction paper and then looks around the room (or outside) to find objects that match the color of their piece of construction paper.

2. When they find an object that matches, child brings the object to a designated area and places it next to the construction-paper piece.

3. After a few moments, review the matches with the children.

4. Continue as time and interest allow.

PRESCHOOL SKILLS

- Color identification
- Color matching

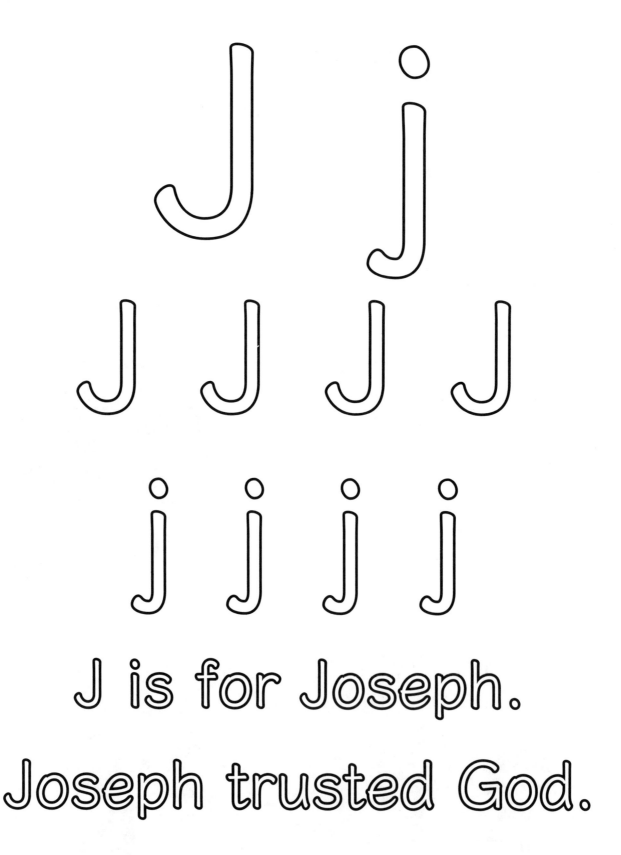

J is for Joseph.

Joseph trusted God.

COLORING PAGE

J is for Joseph.

Joseph's dad gave him a colorful coat.
His brothers were jealous, so
they all took a vote.
They sent Joe to Egypt where
he served others well.
With God by his side, Joseph
was able to excel.

K Is for King Solomon

1 Kings 3

INTRODUCTION

King David was a man after God's own heart. He loved the Lord and loved to read Scripture. King David must have taught his son, Solomon well, because Solomon also grew up to love God and God's Word. One day, the Lord spoke to Solomon and told Solomon he would give him whatever he asked for. What would you ask for if God gave you the same opportunity? Solomon wanted to know how to be a good leader. He asked the Lord for wisdom. God was pleased with Solomon's request and gave him wisdom, respect, and riches.

OPENING ACTIVITY

SOLOMON SAYS

WHAT YOU SAY

When Solomon was talking to the Lord, he said he did not know how to be a leader. The Lord gave his wisdom so that he could be a good king. In this game, we will all practice following the instructions of a leader like Solomon. If I say, "Solomon says," then do what I say. If I don't say, "Solomon says," DON'T do the action!

WHAT YOU DO

1. Play a game like Simon Says. Give children simple instructions to follow (hop on one foot, put your hand on your head, stomp your feet, clap your hands, nod your head, etc.). Act out the instruction.

2. Begin most of the instructions with "Solomon says." Children follow directions.

3. Every now and then throw in an instruction that does NOT begin with "Solomon says." Any child that follows the instruction is out.

TEACHING TIP: When a child is "out," don't make them remain out if they want to play. It's hard for little ones to sit still, and the purpose of the game is to have fun—not to find a winner.

THE BIBLE STORY

1 Kings 3

One night, a King named Solomon was worshiping the Lord. After he went to bed that night, God appeared to him in a dream and said, "Solomon, ask for anything you want, and I will give it to you."

Solomon was surprised! King Solomon knew that his father, David, was a good king. He knew that David followed God's commands. Solomon wanted to do the same thing, but he wasn't sure if he knew how. Solomon prayed to God, "I'm very young and know so little about being a leader. And now I must rule your chosen people, even though there are too many of them to count. Please make me wise and teach me the difference between right and wrong. Then I will know how to rule your people."

God was very pleased with King Solomon's request. Solomon could have asked for riches or for a long life, but he did not. Solomon knew that wisdom is more valuable than riches (Proverbs 16:16). Because Solomon asked for wisdom, God granted his request and also gave him riches. God also promised Solomon that if obeyed God as his father, King David did, Solomon would have a long life.

Solomon used his wisdom to make good decisions in his kingdom. He would help people settle arguments and work out their problems. People even traveled from great distances to test Solomon with difficult questions. God can help us make good decisions too. He will give us wisdom when we ask.

I WONDER . . .

After the story, read these "wonder" statements and questions out loud to your group. Encourage children to respond.

- I wonder what is was like to be a king. What are some reasons you'd like to be a king? Are there any reasons you wouldn't want to be a king?

- I wonder if David was pleased with the decisions his son Solomon was making. If you were Solomon's parent, what would please you about Solomon's decisions?

- I wonder how people heard about Solomon's great wisdom. Why do you think people would have talked about Solomon's wisdom?

- What do you wonder about our Bible story?

ALPHABET REVIEW

Take a few minutes to go over the letters you have recently learned and the Bible stories that go with them. You can use the coloring pages from each week as a timeline and to aid in reviewing.

OPTIONAL EXTRA ACTIVITIES

KING'S CROWN

WHAT YOU NEED

- Yellow or orange construction paper
- Black marker
- Scissors
- Stapler
- Decorative materials (stickers, crayons, markers, glitter glue, etc.)

WHAT YOU DO

1. Children fold a piece of construction paper in half lengthwise and draw a zigzag line along the fold. This will become the top of the crown.

2. Children cut along the zigzag line, creating two pieces.

3. Staple the two parts together.

4. Use the stapled crown to measure around each child's head. Trim the length accordingly.

5. Children decorate crowns with decorative materials.

6. When crowns are decorated, staple the ends to form a crown.

PRESCHOOL SKILLS

- Scissor skills
- Fine-motor skills

SOLOMON BUILDS A TEMPLE

WHAT YOU NEED

- Blocks

WHAT YOU SAY

One thing that Solomon did when he was king was build a temple for God to live in. A temple is a place where people worship God—like our church! Let's work together to build a temple like Solomon did.

WHAT YOU DO

1. Children work together to build a structure like a temple. Talk with them about the various rooms and their shapes.

PRESCHOOL SKILLS

- Pretending
- Working together
- Building
- Hand-eye coordination
- Identifying shapes

SEARCHING FOR WISDOM LIKE HIDDEN TREASURE

WHAT YOU NEED

- Small gold or silver paper plates, at least three for each child (available at most party stores)

WHAT YOU PREPARE

Before children arrive, hide the gold or silver paper-plate "coins" around the room. Make sure there are at least three coins per child hidden.

WHAT YOU DO

1. When it is time, children search for the coins.
2. When coins are found, count all the coins together.

WHAT YOU SAY

King Solomon was a very wise man. Not only did he use his wisdom to make good decisions, he also wrote a lot about it in the book of Proverbs. One verse (Proverbs 2:4) tells us that we should search for wisdom like silver or like hidden treasure—just like you guys did!

PRESCHOOL SKILLS

- Color identification
- Using sense of sight
- Counting
- Identifying circle shape

GLITTERY WISDOM

WHAT YOU NEED

- Word of Wisdom, page 90
- Liquid glue
- Small paper plates
- Cotton swabs
- Glitter

Optional

- Smocks or paint shirts, one for each child

WHAT YOU PREPARE

For each child, make a copy of
Word of Wisdom. Pour a small
amount of glue onto a paper plate and place it near each child.

WHAT YOU DO

OPTIONAL: Children put on smocks or paint shirts.

1. Give each child a cotton swab.

2. Children dip the cotton swab into the glue and then "paint" inside the letters of the word "Wisdom".

3. When they are done "painting", sprinkle the whole page with glitter.

4. The glitter should stick to the glue making the word "wisdom" sparkly and bright.

PRESCHOOL
SKILLS

- Scissor skills
- Fine-motor skills

K is for King Solomon.

King Solomon
was wise.

K is for King Solomon.

King Solomon went to sleep one
night and had a dream.
God told Solomon he could ask for anything.
Solomon asked for wisdom, to be a good king.
God was very pleased and
gave him everything.

L Is for Lion

Daniel 6

INTRODUCTION

Daniel was a man of courage. He is most widely known for his journey into (and out of!) the lions' den in Daniel 6. But Daniel was standing up and doing what was right long before that fateful day. Taken from his home at a young age, Daniel had the courage to refuse the king's food and eat only what was acceptable for God's people (Daniel 1). Daniel continued to grow in his faith through prayer (Daniel 2:18) and was used by God in powerful ways in a foreign land. Perhaps his greatest act of courage (that we know of) was when he refused to give up praying to the one true God and, as a consequence, was faced with a pit full of hungry lions.

OPENING ACTIVITY

WHAT DOES THE LION SAY?

WHAT YOU NEED

- Animal Cards, page 15
- Scissors or paper cutter

WHAT YOU PREPARE

Make a copy of the Animal Cards and cut them apart. Place cards face down on a table.

WHAT YOU DO

1. Select a card and imitate the noise made by the animal on the card.

2. Children guess which animal is on the card. The child who first guesses correctly chooses a card and makes the noise made by that animal. Be prepared to help children make noises.

3. Continue until all the cards have been guessed or as time and interest allow.

WHAT YOU SAY

In our true story today, a man named Daniel spent some time with some animals. Can you guess what animals they were? The animals made this sound . . . (Roar.) Now can you guess? (Children respond.) You're right! Daniel spent time with a bunch of lions. Even though lions are lovely to look at and may seem like fun, they are actually very dangerous creatures. Daniel could have gotten hurt by being that close to the lions, but God protected Daniel.

THE BIBLE STORY

Daniel 6

Once, long ago, there was a man named Daniel who lived in a city called Babylon. Even though Daniel was one of God's people, he did not get to live with the rest of God's people. He lived in a different place far away. Sometimes it was hard to do the right thing.

Daniel did his best to stay close to God by praying and following God's commandments. Daniel was brave throughout his whole life, but there was one time when Daniel showed an amazing amount of courage.

In Babylon, Daniel was a leader. He was a helper of the king, but many of the other helpers did not like Daniel. They decided to do something to get Daniel in trouble. They asked the king to make it a rule that no one could pray to anyone except for the king. This meant that Daniel could not pray to the one true God!

The king agreed to the rule and said if anyone disobeyed that he would be thrown into a den of hungry lions. Daniel had a tough choice to make. Would he obey God or would he obey the king?

Daniel was brave. He chose to obey God and continued to pray to him. Daniel was thrown in the lion's den. He should have been eaten up right away, but God protected Daniel. God is powerful and strong. Daniel trusted God and we can trust God, too.

I WONDER . . .

After the story, read these "wonder" statements and questions out loud to your group. Encourage children to respond.

- I wonder why the king agreed to the rule that made people pray to him. Who is it OK to pray to?

- I wonder if Daniel was afraid of going into the lions' den. How would you feel if you were Daniel? What would your face look like?

- I wonder if there is ever a time when you need courage from God. What could you do if you needed God's help to feel courage?

- What do you wonder about our Bible story?

ALPHABET REVIEW

Take a few minutes to go over the letters you have recently learned and the Bible stories that go with them. You can use the coloring pages from each week as a timeline and to aid in reviewing.

OPTIONAL EXTRA ACTIVITIES

PRAYER CARDS

WHAT YOU NEED

- Prayer Cards, page 98
- Scissors
- Resealable plastic sandwich bags

WHAT YOU PREPARE

For each child, make a copy of the Prayer Cards.

WHAT YOU SAY

Daniel knew that prayer was important. Prayer is one way we can be friends with God. Today, we are going to pray to the one true God, using these cards to help us.

What You Do

1. Children use scissors to cut along the solid lines. Help children as needed.

2. When cards have been cut, children pick out one or two cards.

3. Lead children to take turns praying, using the cards to prompt them what to pray for.

4. When activity is done, children put the cards inside a resealable plastic sandwich bag to take home.

PRESCHOOL SKILLS

- **Communicating needs**
- **Scissor skills**

PAPER-PLATE LION FACE

WHAT YOU NEED

- Paper plates (not Styrofoam)
- Yellow, orange, and brown construction paper
- Scissors
- Glue
- Packing tape or duct tape
- Craft sticks

WHAT YOU PREPARE

For each child, cut out the center of a paper plate to make an opening for a mask.

WHAT YOU DO

1. Each child cuts a piece of construction paper into strips. When the strips are cut, put them in the middle of the table.

2. Children glue the construction-paper strips around the outside of the paper plate to create a lion's mane.

3. Use the packing tape or duct tape to secure a craft stick on the bottom of the mask to serve as a handle.

4. Children hold their masks over their faces, roar, and pretend to be lions.

PRESCHOOL SKILLS

- **Scissor skills**
- **Working together**

LITTLE PEOPLE THEATRE

WHAT YOU NEED

- Toy people
- Toy lions

WHAT YOU DO

1. Children use toy people and lions and work together to retell the Bible story.

PRESCHOOL SKILLS

- **Recall and retelling a story**
- **Working together**

RUNNING FROM THE LIONS

WHAT YOU DO

1. Children play a game like Sharks and Minnows. Children stand against one wall.

2. Select two children to be "lions" and stand in the middle of the room.

3. On your signal, children standing against a wall try to run to the opposite wall without getting tagged by a "lion."

4. If children get tagged, they sit down.

TEACHING TIP: When a child is "out," don't make them remain out if they want to play. It's hard for little ones to sit still, and the purpose of the game is to have fun—not to find a winner.

WHAT YOU SAY

It was hard not to get tagged by a lion in this game. In real life, we couldn't outrun a lion. There was no way Daniel could have escaped the lions in the den without God's help. God is powerful and strong. We can always trust him.

PRESCHOOL SKILLS

- Gross-motor skills

L is for Lion.

God saved Daniel
from the lions.

L is for lion.

Daniel prayed to God, both night and day
Even when the bad guys tried
to make him disobey
Daniel trusted God when
thrown to hungry beasts
The lions did not eat him, and
Daniel was released.

PRAYER CARDS

M Is for Moses

Exodus

INTRODUCTION

Moses was an unlikely hero. When he was born, the king of Egypt, Pharaoh, was trying to get rid of all the Hebrew babies (Exodus 1). These were God's chosen people. Moses' mother saved him by hiding him, placing him in a basket and the basket in the river. He was found by the Egyptian princess who raised him. Later, after Moses discovered who he really was, he fled to the desert. Eventually, Moses returned to Egypt and became a great leader to his people. After God demonstrated his might power, Pharaoh let God's people leave Egypt. However, when God's people reach the Red Sea, they realized Pharaoh and his army were coming after them. Pharaoh had changed his mind! What were the people going to do?

OPENING ACTIVITY

SEPARATING WATER

WHAT YOU NEED

- Large bowl of water
- Towels

WHAT YOU DO

1. Children examine the bowl of water, and put their hands in it, trying to separate the water.

WHAT YOU SAY

Ask children to try to separate the water into two halves. **Can you keep the water from touching? Water is a funny thing. We can't move it like other things because it is a liquid. We can't cut down through it with our hands. We can't keep it from touching. However, in our true story today, God did the impossible. He did something with water that we could never do!**

THE BIBLE STORY

Genesis 50

God's people had lived for a long time in a land called Egypt. When Joseph was in charge (Genesis 50), God's people were treated well. However, after Joseph died, a new Pharaoh became king and he did not like God's people. He treated them poorly and made them work very hard.

God's people prayed and asked God to rescue them. God sent Moses to rescue them. God also sent many disasters on the land of Egypt to show how powerful he was. Pharaoh finally let God's people go. The people were so happy! They were going to a new land and would be able to worship God there. However, it wasn't long until they had some trouble on their journey.

God's people had stopped to camp by a sea. Soon, the people looked up and saw Pharaoh and his armies coming after them. They were very scared. They prayed and asked God to help them.

Moses told the people to be calm because God would fight for them. God told Moses to stretch out his hand over the water. When Moses obeyed, the water split into two parts! There was a wall of water on the right and wall of water on the left and a path right in the middle! It was amazing.

God's people crossed through the sea on dry land. When they had all safely reached the other side, God closed the water again behind them. God's people were safe. He had rescued them.

I WONDER . . .

After the story, read these "wonder" statements and questions out loud to your group. Encourage children to respond.

- I wonder how God's people felt as they went through the sea. What do you think it would be like to walk on a path with tall walls of water on either side?

- I wonder if Moses was afraid that Pharaoh would catch them. How do you think you would have felt?

- I wonder what the people thought after they had made it safely to the other side. What would be the first thing you'd do?

- What do you wonder about our Bible story?

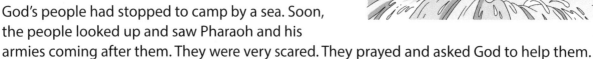

ALPHABET REVIEW

Take a few minutes to go over the letters you have recently learned and the Bible stories that go with them. You can use the coloring pages from each week as a timeline and to aid in reviewing.

OPTIONAL EXTRA ACTIVITIES

PYRAMIDS

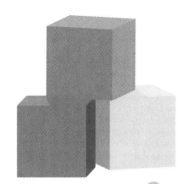

WHAT YOU NEED

- Books with photos or illustrations of Egypt pyramids or pictures of pyramids printed from the Internet
- Blocks

WHAT YOU SAY

Hold up pictures of pyramids from Egypt. **God's people had to work hard to build these giant pyramids!**

WHAT YOU DO

1. Children use blocks to build pyramids like the ones they see in the pictures.
2. When children finish a pyramid, count how many blocks are in it.

PRESCHOOL SKILLS

- Fine-motor skills
- Identifying shapes
- Counting
- Working together

STORY SEQUENCE

WHAT YOU NEED

- Red Sea Story Cards, page 106
- Scissors or paper cutter

WHAT YOU PREPARE

Make a copy of the Red Sea Story Cards and cut them apart. Spread out the cards on the floor or a table.

WHAT YOU SAY

Each of these pictures show a part of the story. Work together to put the story in order. There are numbers at the bottom of the cards to help!

WHAT YOU DO

1. Children work together to put the story cards in order.
2. Read the words on each card to help children.

PRESCHOOL SKILLS

- Sorting
- Understanding and retelling a story
- Counting
- Working together

FISH IN THE SEA SNACK

WHAT YOU NEED

- Graham crackers
- Spoon
- Blue frosting
- Paper plates
- Plastic knives
- Fish snacks (Goldfish crackers, Swedish fish candies, etc.)

WHAT YOU PREPARE

Place a spoonful of blue frosting on a graham cracker and place cracker on a paper plate. Prepare one cracker for each child.

WHAT YOU DO

1. Children use plastic knives to spread the frosting on their graham crackers.

2. After they are done frosting, allow them to put two or three fish snacks on the cracker.

WHAT YOU SAY

What is there about our snack that reminds you of the Bible story?

PRESCHOOL SKILLS

- Color identification
- Counting

RED SEA SENSORY BAG

WHAT YOU NEED

- Gallon-sized resealable plastic bag
- Small fish beads
- Hair gel
- Blue food coloring
- Packing tape

WHAT YOU PREPARE

Partially fill a freezer bag with hair gel and add blue food coloring and beads. Squeeze as much air out of the bag as you can and then seal shut. Tape the opening closed to secure.

WHAT YOU SAY

Imagine this is the Red Sea. See if you can make a path through the pretend Re Sea with their fingers.

WHAT YOU DO

1. Children move the gel with their fingers.

TEACHER TIP: Prepare more than one bag for children to play with. Or prepare one sandwich-sized bag for each child.

PRESCHOOL SKILLS

- **Pretend play**
- **Recreating a story**
- **Pre-writing skills**

M m

M M M M

m m m m

M is for Moses.
Moses trusted God.

M is for Moses.

Moses led God's people towards the Red Sea
They could not get across, it
was much too deep.
Moses prayed to God, he knew
God was the boss.
God parted the waters so the
people then could cross.

Pharaoh treated God's people badly.

(1)

God's people prayed to God and asked him to help.

(2)

God's people were able to leave Egypt. They set up camp by the Red Sea.

(3)

God rescued his people by parting the waters so the people could walk across on dry ground.

(4)

N Is for Nehemiah

Nehemiah 1–2, 4, 6:15

INTRODUCTION

Nehemiah was one of God's chosen people, but he was not living in God's Promised Land. Many of God's people had been taken away to different lands. One day, Nehemiah heard news about Jerusalem, the land where God's people used to live. He heard the walls had been torn down and everything was in disrepair. This made Nehemiah so sad. Nehemiah's job was to serve drinks to the king. When Nehemiah took the king his drink, the king noticed that Nehemiah was sad. When Nehemiah explained the situation, the king sent Nehemiah back to his hometown to rebuild the walls.

OPENING ACTIVITY

GATHERING SUPPLIES

WHAT YOU NEED

- One sheet of construction paper in each of four colors: red, yellow, green, blue
- Several building blocks, at least five each in red, yellow, green, blue

WHAT YOU PREPARE

Scatter the building blocks around the room. Lay the four pieces of construction paper on a table.

WHAT YOU SAY

Nehemiah had a big job—rebuilding walls around his hometown. What do you think Nehemiah would need to build this wall? (Children respond.) **Let's pretend we're gathering up supplies.**

WHAT YOU DO

1. Children find the blocks and then place them on the matching paper.
2. When all the blocks are found, count the blocks together.

THE BIBLE STORY

Nehemiah 1–2, 4, 6:15

Have you ever worked very hard on a project? Have you ever built something that was tall and strong? Nehemiah had a big project to do. He wanted to rebuild the walls that were all around Jerusalem.

God's people used to live in Jerusalem, but many had moved away or been taken to different lands. Nehemiah wanted to fix the walls so God's people could come back home. When Nehemiah heard about the broken-down walls, he was working for a king in a faraway land. The king noticed Nehemiah was sad and told Nehemiah he could return home to fix the walls.

At first, many people joined Nehemiah in the work. They were excited about fixing the wall around their home. But soon, the work grew very difficult. It was hard to sort through all the broken rocks.

Other people came and teased the workers. They said the walls were weak and would fall over if even a fox jumped on them (Nehemiah 4:3). Nehemiah told the people to trust in God and keep working.

The mean people came back and said they would knock down the walls. Nehemiah was determined to keep working. He told God's people to carry a sword or spear and protect the wall as they were working on it.

The people continued to work hard and soon the wall was completed. It was a big project, but the people worked hard. With God's help, they were able to finish the wall.

I WONDER . . .

After the story, read these "wonder" statements and questions out loud to your group. Encourage children to respond.

● I wonder how God's people felt as they began work on the wall. What kinds of feelings do you think they had?

● I wonder why the king allowed Nehemiah to leave?

● I wonder what God's people were feeling when people began to tease them?

● What do you wonder about our Bible story?

● ● ● ● ● ● ● ● ● ● ●

ALPHABET REVIEW

Take a few minutes to go over the letters you have recently learned and the Bible stories that go with them. You can use the coloring pages from each week as a timeline and to aid in reviewing.

OPTIONAL EXTRA ACTIVITIES

TASTE TEST

WHAT YOU NEED

- Varieties of juice
- Small paper cups
- Bucket

TEACHER TIP: Be sure to post a note for parents about allergies before doing this activity.

WHAT YOU SAY

Before Nehemiah began work on the wall, he worked for a king. He was the cupbearer to the king. A cupbearer tastes the king's drinks to make sure they are OK. Today, we're going to do some taste-testing too!

WHAT YOU DO

1. Give each child a cup and pour a little juice in it.

2. Children taste the juice and decide whether it is "okay" or not. Children either finish the juice in their cups or pour the remainder into the bucket.

3. Repeat the process with another kind of juice. Ask children about what juice was their favorite.

PRESCHOOL SKILLS

- **Using the sense of taste**

CONSTRUCTION ZONE DRAMATIC PLAY

WHAT YOU NEED

- Large blocks
- Toy construction tools
- Tape measure
- Construction hats

WHAT YOU PREPARE

Using the above listed supplies, set up a dramatic play zone for children to explore.

WHAT YOU DO

1. Children build together as time and interest allow.

PRESCHOOL SKILLS

- **Dramatic Play**
- **Motor Skills**
- **Understanding positions of objects**
- **Working together**

PRAYER WALL

WHAT YOU NEED

- White paper
- Crayons or markers
- Way to post things on a wall (sticky tack, tape, etc.)

WHAT YOU SAY

Nehemiah prayed to God when he needed help building the wall. What is something you can ask God to help you with? Today we're going to draw a picture of something we could use God's help with.

WHAT YOU DO

1. Children draw pictures of things they need God's help with.
2. Post finished pictures on the wall.
3. As a group, pray for each of the pictures.

PRESCHOOL SKILLS

- Empathy
- Fine-motor skills
- Drawing

PUTTING IT TOGETHER

WHAT YOU NEED

- Wall Puzzle, page 113
- Crayons or markers
- Scissors
- Resealable plastic bag, one for each child

WHAT YOU SAY

As Nehemiah and his friends were working on the wall, some people came and made fun of them. They did not want Nehemiah to finish the wall, so they threatened to attack God's people and tear down the wall (Nehemiah 4:16–19). **Nehemiah told God's people to carry a sword with them and keep on building!**

WHAT YOU PREPARE

For each child, make a copy of the Wall Puzzle.

WHAT YOU DO

1. Children color the wall and the words.
2. Cut out the puzzle pieces and then put them together again.
3. Children put puzzle pieces in resealable plastic bag to take home.

PRESCHOOL SKILLS

- Scissor skills
- Fine-motor skills
- Improving hand-eye coordination

N n

N N N N N

n n n n n

N is for Nehemiah.

Nehemiah built the wall.

Instant Bible Lessons for Preschoolers: A to Z Thru the Bible

N is for Nehemiah.

Nehemiah heard the walls of his
home had fallen down.
This made Nehemiah very sad,
and he wore a frown.
Nehemiah worked hard to
rebuild the fallen wall.
With God's help, soon the walls
were standing strong and tall.

WALL PUZZLE

God helped the people rebuild the walls

O Is for Obey

2 Kings 18:1–12

INTRODUCTION

All throughout Scripture, we see a common theme: Obedience brings blessings and disobedience brings destruction (or other bad consequences). This is a guiding principle we use when raising children. As parents, we teach our children to obey in order to protect them from harm and destruction. God had created the family structure in order to help children understand right from wrong. When children are young, they learn to obey their parents and teachers. Later, this foundation of obedience will help them to listen to and obey God as well. Today, we will look at a king in Israel's history who worked hard to obey God. Because of his obedience, God brought many blessings into King Hezekiah's life.

OPENING ACTIVITY

RED LIGHT, GREEN LIGHT

WHAT YOU NEED

- Two sheets of construction pape, one red and one green

WHAT YOU DO

1. For the first round, be "It." "It" the red paper in one hand and the green paper in the other.

2. The remaining players stand a good distance away from "It."

3. "It" turns their back on the other players, holds up the green paper, and calls out, "Green light!" The other players move towards "It."

4. After a moment, "It" spins around, holds up red paper, and calls, "Red light."

5. When they hear "Red light," the other players freeze. Any child seen moving must return to the starting place.

6. Players remain frozen until "It" turns around again, holds up the green paper and calls out "Green Light."

1. Play continues until someone tags "It." The tagger becomes the new "It." Assist "It" with turning, holding up appropriate paper and calling out commands.

2. Play continues as time and interest allow.

WHAT YOU SAY

It isn't always easy to obey right away, is it? God has commanded us to obey our parents, but it's not always easy. However, when we do obey, we get blessings in our lives. Sometimes our parents can do fun things with us, or sometimes obeying keeps us from getting hurt. Obedience always leads to blessings.

THE BIBLE STORY

2 Kings 18:1–12

God gave us the Bible so we can learn how to live. It teaches us the right thing to do. In the Bible, there is a true story about a man named Hezekiah.

Hezekiah was a king who loved God. Hezekiah tried hard to do the right thing and to obey God. Because King Hezekiah obeyed God, God gave him many blessings. The king was successful in whatever he did (2 Kings 18:7). When the king went to battle, God helped him to win.

God wants us to obey as well. God wants us to obey the Bible just like King Hezekiah did. When we are little, we don't always understand what the Bible says. That's why we have parents, grandparents, and teachers who can help us read and understand the Bible.

When we obey our parents, we are learning to obey God as well. When we obey our parents, we are able to do good things. Obedience brings blessings. We can obey even when it's hard.

I WONDER . . .

After the story, read these "wonder" statements and questions out loud to your group. Encourage children to respond.

- I wonder why Hezekiah loved God so much. Why do you love God?
- I wonder why it is hard to sometimes obey. Can you think of a reason it might be hard to obey?
- I wonder why God gave us parents. Why do you think God wants us to obey our parents?
- What do you wonder about our Bible story?

ALPHABET REVIEW

Take a few minutes to go over the letters you have recently learned and the Bible stories that go with them. You can use the coloring pages from each week as a timeline and to aid in reviewing.

OPTIONAL EXTRA ACTIVITIES

I CHOSE TO OBEY

WHAT YOU NEED

- Construction paper
- Crayons or markers

WHAT YOU DO

1. Children draw a picture showing a way that they can obey.

2. Help them print their name in large letters on the top of the page followed by the words "chooses to obey."

WHAT YOU SAY

Remember you can obey their parents and teachers every day. Be sure to practice obedience this week. God is happy when you obey!

PRESCHOOL SKILLS

- **Recognizing first name in print**
- **Printing first name**

LET'S PRACTICE OBEDIENCE!

WHAT YOU NEED

- Index cards
- Marker or pen

WHAT YOU PREPARE

Print simple instructions for tasks around the room. Some suggested tasks are: pick up three toys, toss a ball to a friend, jump on one foot, pick up a book and put it away, give a toy to a friend, hug a friend, touch your nose, jump up and down, etc.

WHAT YOU DO

1. Children take turns selecting a card. Read instruction aloud.

2. Children obey the instruction on the card.

3. Praise kids with great enthusiasm when they obey.

PRESCHOOL SKILLS

- **Motor skills**
- **Listening to and obeying simple instructions**

IN A HAPPY WAY

WHAT YOU NEED

- Happy Cards, page 120

WHAT YOU PREPARE

Make a copy of the Happy Cards and cut cards apart. Put cards into two piles: one pile for actions and one piles for feelings.

WHAT YOU DO

1. Children pick one card from each pile and act them out. For example, if they pick the "grumpy" card and "baking cookies", they should pretend to bake cookies with a grumpy face.

2. The other children guess what they are acting out.

WHAT YOU SAY

Talk with children about whether the person was obeying with a happy heart.

PRESCHOOL SKILLS

- Dramatic play
- Motor Skills
- Understanding emotions

DRAMATIC PLAY

WHAT YOU NEED

- Home living toys
- Toy cars
- Dress-up clothes

WHAT YOU SAY

We have an opportunity to practice obedience many times each day. We can obey our parents at home, when we are out walking around, and any time! Today, you can dress up and some of you can pretend to be the parents and some of you can pretend to be the children. Let's practice obedience as we play.

WHAT YOU DO

1. Children explore the home-living toys, toy cars, and dress-up clothes.

2. Encourage children to act out ways to obey.

PRESCHOOL SKILLS

- Dramatic Play
- Working with others

O is for obey.

I can obey my parents.

O is for obey.

God gave us parents so we can learn
What to do at every turn.
God clearly told us to obey
As mom and dad help show us the way.

Grumpy

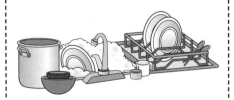

Wash dishes

Bake cookies

Happy

Feed the pet

Rake the leaves

Sad

Shovel snow

Go on a walk

Mad

Read to a friend

Clean up toys

Confused

Carry bags

Wash window

P Is for Paul

Acts 9, 27, 28

INTRODUCTION

Paul was a man who truly changed the world through his words and actions. Originally a man who hated Christians, Paul's heart was changed when God spoke to him from the heavens one day (Acts 9). After that, Paul spent his life sharing the gospel, traveling to visit Christians, and writing to encourage people to grow in their faith. He is responsible for writing much of the New Testament and the letters he wrote to the early churches provide wonderful instruction for us all.

OPENING ACTIVITY

GOING ON A TRIP

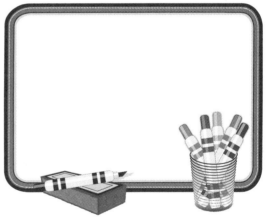

WHAT YOU NEED

- Dry-erase board and markers or large sheet of paper and markers

WHAT YOU SAY

A long time ago, there was a man named Paul. Paul loved God and wanted to tell other people about him. Paul traveled often to visit new lands and tell people about Jesus. Of course, whenever you go on a trip, you've got to do some packing!

WHAT YOU DO

1. Ask children what things they would pack if they were going on a big trip. Write down the named items (or even better—draw quick pictures!).

2. After a few responses, ask children what Paul might have taken on a trip. Explain that travel would have looked very different in Paul's time. There were no airplanes, cars, or trains. People traveled on foot or by boat for the most part. Talk about what difficulties Paul might have experienced as he traveled.

THE BIBLE STORY

Acts 9, 27, 28

Have you ever gotten a card or letter in the mail? Who was it from? Paul was a man who loved God very much. He wanted to share the good news of Jesus with everyone. One way he did this was by writing letters. Paul wrote letters to churches that he had visited to encourage them to love God, do the right thing, and help others around them.

Paul did not have an easy life. The leaders in his time would often get mad at Paul for telling other people about God. In fact, sometimes they would even put him in prison! Still, Paul continued to tell everyone he could about how much Jesus loves us.

One time, Paul was traveling by boat with many other men. This was no ordinary journey. Paul was a prisoner! Even though Paul was being taken to a jail, he still showed kindness to everyone on the boat. He helped them make good choices and prayed to God for protection.

The boat was destroyed in a big storm, but because of God's protection, everyone on board made it safely to a nearby island. Even on the island, Paul wanted to tell the people about God. Paul was bitten by a snake, but he did not get sick. Paul explained that God had protected him. After this, the island people brought many of the sick to Paul so he could pray for them. God healed many people on that island.

God is amazing and powerful and it is so exciting to tell other people about him.

I WONDER . . .

After the story, read these "wonder" statements and questions out loud to your group. Encourage children to respond.

- I wonder how Paul felt when he was traveling on the boat during the storm. How do you think Paul felt? How do you think the other people on the boat felt?

- I wonder why Paul dedicated so much of his life to writing letters to others. Why do you think Paul wrote letters?

- I wonder why Paul kept on telling people about God even though it sometimes caused him trouble (people hurt him or put him in jail). Why do you think Paul kept telling people about God?

- What do you wonder about our Bible story?

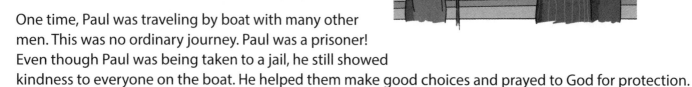

ALPHABET REVIEW

Take a few minutes to go over the letters you have recently learned and the Bible stories that go with them. You can use the coloring pages from each week as a timeline and to aid in reviewing.

OPTIONAL EXTRA ACTIVITIES

SPECIAL DELIVERY!

WHAT YOU NEED

- Large cardboard box
- Scissors or utility knife
- Postcards
- Blank paper
- Envelopes
- Stickers
- Crayons or markers

WHAT YOU PREPARE

Close cardboard box. Use scissors or utility knife to cut a slit in one side of the box.

WHAT YOU SAY

In Paul's time, letters were carried by hand by a messenger. Nowadays, we have a whole system to help us deliver mail. In this activity, we're going to pretend to be delivery people and bring mail to each other.

WHAT YOU DO

1. Children "write letters" by writing or scribbling on sheets of blank paper or postcards. Help children print their names on letters or postcards, if they are able.

2. If using sheets of paper, children fold papers, put them in an envelope and seal the envelope.

3. Children place stickers on envelopes or postcards as stamps.

4. Children carry letters and postcards to each other or drop them in the slit in the box.

PRESCHOOL SKILLS

- Dramatic play
- Pre-writing skills
- Printing first name

PRAYER JAR

WHAT YOU NEED

- Prayer Jar Papers, page 128
- Crayons or markers
- Scissors
- Small plastic jar, one per child
- Tape
- Jumbo craft sticks

WHAT YOU PREPARE

For each child, make a copy of Prayer Jar Papers.

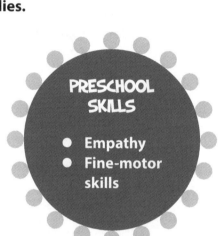

WHAT YOU SAY

Paul spent a lot of time praying for others. We can pray for others, too. Let's make a prayer jar we can take home to pray with our families.

WHAT YOU DO

1. Children color jar label and parent note and then cut them out.

2. Children tape label to jar and then place parent note inside.

3. Children decorate craft sticks. As they are working on their project, brainstorm with the children about possible prayer requests.

4. Children take the jars home to use every day to pray for others with their family.

PRESCHOOL SKILLS

- **Empathy**
- **Fine-motor skills**

PAUL SHOWS LOVE FOR OTHERS

WHAT YOU NEED

- Washable paint
- Paper plates (not Styrofoam)
- Paper-towel or toilet-paper tubes
- White construction paper or cardstock

Optional

- Smocks or paint shirts, one for each child

WHAT YOU PREPARE

Pour a little bit of paint onto the paper plates and place on a table. Bend cardboard tubes a bit so that they form the shape of a heart.

WHAT YOU DO

OPTIONAL: Children put on smocks or paint shirts.

1. Children dip the tubes into the paint and then use them like a stamp to put hearts on their sheet of paper or cardstock.

WHAT YOU SAY

Our hearts remind us that Paul loved both God and others.

PACKING A SUITCASE RELAY RACE

WHAT YOU NEED

- Two suitcases or duffel bags
- Various articles of clothing

WHAT YOU PREPARE

Place the suitcases or duffel bags at one end of the room and the pile of clothing at the other end.

WHAT YOU DO

1. Children divide into two teams and line up next to the pile of clothes.

2. At your signal, the first player on each team picks up a piece of clothing, runs to their team suitcase or bag, and puts clothing inside the bag.

3. Player returns to their team, tags the next person, and goes to the end of the line.

4. Game continues until everyone has a turn or every item in the clothing pile gets packed.

P p

P P P P

p p p p

P is for Paul.

Paul loved God and others.

P is for Paul.

Paul loved God, we know that is true.
He shared about Jesus and we can too.
Paul wrote letters and prayed for friends.
He taught us that on God we can depend.

Parents: Print prayer requests on craft sticks and keep in this jar. When you pray with your family, use prayer sticks as reminders what to lift up to God. When a prayer is answered, print the way God answered the prayer on the other side of the stick and store in a second "Answered Prayers" jar.

Q Is for Queen Esther

INTRODUCTION

The book of Esther contains an absolutely fascinating account of God's perfect timing and how coincidences are not always what they seem. In this Biblical story, a young Jewish girl is unexpectedly chosen to be queen. While this may seem like a dream come true for many girls, Esther was not so sure she was up to the responsibility of being a leader to the people. When she was faced with a difficult decision early in her reign, Esther went to God in prayer.

OPENING ACTIVITY

BEAUTY TREATMENTS

WHAT YOU NEED

● Different types of lotions

WHAT YOU SAY

A long time ago, there was a king who was in need of a queen. Many ladies went to the palace in hopes of being chosen as the next queen. Before they could meet the king, each lady went through twelve months of preparation. This included using lotions, perfumes, make-up, and other things. Today, we're going to smell some lotions and maybe even try a few on! Which fragrance do you like best? What do you think the lotions in Esther's day were made from?

WHAT YOU DO

1. Children sniff the different lotions and put a bit on their hands and arms if they wish.

THE BIBLE STORY

Many years ago, there was a king named Xerses who was in need of a queen. Many ladies in the land wanted to be the next queen, but only one girl would be chosen.

Esther loved God and wanted to obey him, but she wasn't sure how being queen would fit into God's plan. Esther was kind to everyone she met and made friends with many people. Even the king himself liked Esther better than any of the other girls and soon chose her to be his queen.

Not long after Esther became queen, she learned of an evil plan from a man named Haman. Haman did not like Esther's people—the Jewish people who were God's chosen people. He wanted all Jewish people killed!

Esther's uncle wanted her to speak to the king about Haman's evil plan, but Esther was afraid. She was not allowed to go to the king without an invitation. What if the king got mad at her? What if he threw her into prison? What if he agreed with Haman?

Esther was confused. She didn't know what do to. She gathered up her close friends and they all spent time praying. They did not eat or drink for three days. They concentrated on praying.

At the end of this time, Esther went to the king. Thankfully, the king was gracious to Esther. He understood why she was upset and he promised to protect her and her people. God's chosen people were saved! Esther was brave even when it was hard because God gave her courage.

I WONDER . . .

After the story, read these "wonder" statements and questions out loud to your group. Encourage children to respond.

- I wonder how Esther felt when she was chosen to be queen. How would you feel if you were chosen to be queen?

- I wonder what Esther did to make other people like her so much. What things make you like someone?

- I wonder why the King listened to Esther instead of Haman. Why do you think the king listened to Esther?

- What do you wonder about our Bible story?

ALPHABET REVIEW

Take a few minutes to go over the letters you have recently learned and the Bible stories that go with them. You can use the coloring pages from each week as a timeline and to aid in reviewing.

OPTIONAL EXTRA ACTIVITIES

GRAGGERS

WHAT YOU NEED

- Toilet-paper tubes, one for each child
- Stapler
- Beans or jingle bells
- Pencils, one per child
- Duct tape

WHAT YOU SAY

In the Jewish tradition, the story of Esther is read every year to the children. Whenever the name "Haman" is said, the children boo or make loud noises because Haman was the bad guy. Today, we're going to make a gragger—which is one thing the children use to make loud noises during the story.

WHAT YOU DO

1. Children color the outside of their toilet-paper tube.

2. Fold the tube in half and staple one end closed.

3. Children place a few bells or beans in the tube.

4. Place a pencil at one corner of the open end and staple closed. Use duct tape to secure the pencil to the tube, and over both ends of the tube.

5. Read the Esther account from a children's Bible or from the previous pages and encourage children to shake their graggers whenever they hear the name "Haman."

PRESCHOOL SKILLS

- **Listening skills**
- **Fine-motor skills**
- **Story comprehension**

LITTLE PEOPLE STORY TIME

WHAT YOU NEED

- Toy people, one for each person in the Bible story

WHAT YOU DO

1. Give each child a toy person and assign them a role from the Bible story. If you have more children than roles, you can add extra roles such as servants or guards.

2. Re-read or re-tell the story as children act out the story using the toy people.

3. Later, children engage in free play using the figures.

PRESCHOOL SKILLS

- Pretend play
- Playing with others
- Story comprehension

KING OR QUEEN FOR A DAY

WHAT YOU NEED

- Robe or cape
- Paper or play crown
- Long cardboard tube (wrapping-paper tube, etc.)

WHAT YOU PREPARE

Set a chair at one end of the play area.

WHAT YOU SAY

Today we heard about Queen Esther and how she needed help from God to ask a favor from her husband, the king. We can pray and ask God for help like Esther did. Let's play a game and pretend to be kings and queens!

PRESCHOOL SKILLS

- Gross-motor skills

WHAT YOU DO

1. Children form a line opposite the chair.

2. Each child takes a turn to put on the robe or cape and the crown, and hold the cardboard tube like a sceptor.

3. Children march regally across the room to sit in the chair "throne," point the cardboard tube at the rest of the children, and then return to the line.

4. Child hand the robe or cape, crown, and cardboard tube to the next child to take a turn.

MASK MAKING

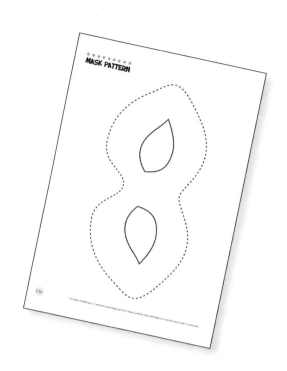

WHAT YOU NEED

- Mask Pattern, page 136
- Colored cardstock
- Scissors
- Decorative items (feathers, gems, markers, glue, stickers, etc.)
- ¼-inch elastic
- Stapler

WHAT YOU PREPARE

For each child, use colored cardstock to make a copy of Mask Pattern.

WHAT YOU SAY

Every year, the Jewish people have a party to celebrate Queen Esther. This holiday is called Purim. People wear masks to the party. Let's make masks we can wear!

WHAT YOU DO

1. Children cut out a mask. Assist children with cutting out the eyes.

2. Children use decorating items to decorate their masks. Talk with children about the colors and shapes of the decorative items on their masks.

3. When the children are done decorating masks, cut a length of elastic and staple to the sides of their mask.

PRESCHOOL SKILLS

- Fine-motor skills
- Color identification
- Identify shapes

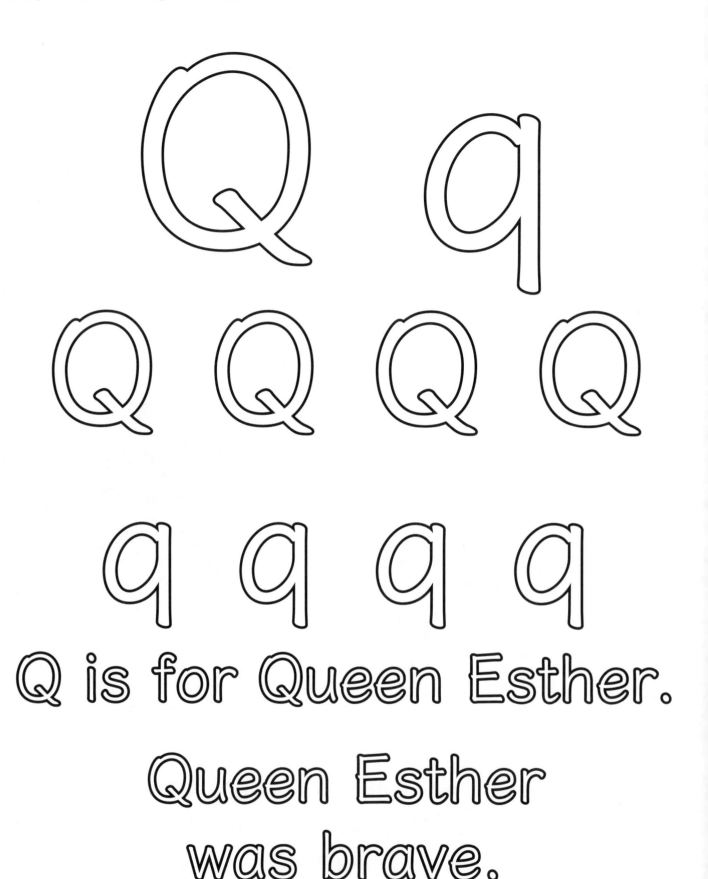

Q is for Queen Esther.

Queen Esther
was brave.

Q is for Queen Esther.

Esther was a young girl, chosen to be queen.
She quickly heard about a
man who was mean.
Haman was bad and wanted to trick the king.
But Esther was brave and told
the king everything.

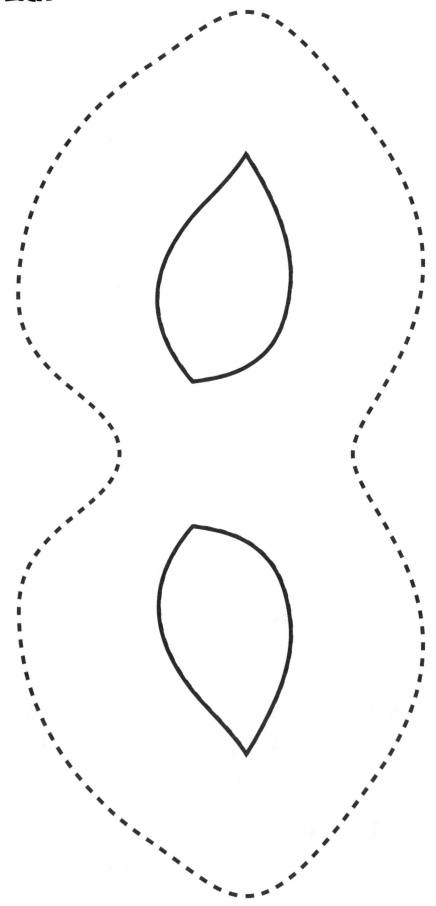

R Is for Ruth

Ruth

INTRODUCTION

Ruth was introduced to the one true God through her husband's mother. When Ruth's husband died, Ruth decided to stay with her mother in-law. Together, these women traveled back to Bethlehem in hopes of finding food and friends. Ruth could have returned to her own home town and found a new husband, but she was faithful to Naomi and trusted that God would provide for them.

OPENING ACTIVITY

TRAVELING TO BETHLEHEM

WHAT YOU NEED

- Small suitcase or duffel bag

WHAT YOU DO

1. Children play a game like Follow the Leader. Select one child to be Naomi and designate them the "Leader." Hand the Leader the small suitcase or duffel bag to carry.

2. The other children pretend that they are "Ruth" and follow Naomi around the room, doing the same actions that she does.

WHAT YOU SAY

This was a fun game to play. Ruth followed Naomi the same way that you all followed our leader. Ruth said that she would go wherever Naomi went and she would worship the one true God just like Naomi did.

THE BIBLE STORY

Ruth

In Bible times, there were often famines in the land. During a famine, crops do not grow and many people are without food. Often, people will travel to different lands in order to find food.

When the food ran out in Moab, Naomi and Ruth traveled to Bethlehem in hopes of finding food. Naomi was getting older and could not do much work, but Ruth was determined to do the best she could.

Early one morning, Ruth began to work in a field that just happened to be owned by a distant relative named Boaz. Ruth was able to pick up the grain that the other workers had left behind. Boaz noticed Ruth and was pleased that she was such a hard worker. He told his workers to leave a little extra grain out for Ruth.

When Ruth returned home, Naomi could not believe how much food Ruth was able to gather! She knew that God had provided for both of them. Naomi encouraged Ruth to continue to work in Boaz's field and Boaz continued to show her kindness. Ruth was happy that God had given her a safe place to gather food.

After the harvest was complete, Naomi encouraged Ruth to speak to Boaz. Boaz admired Ruth and the kindness he had shown to Naomi. He decided to marry her and everyone was very happy.

I WONDER . . .

After the story, read these "wonder" statements and questions out loud to your group. Encourage children to respond.

- I wonder how Naomi felt as she journeyed back to her homeland. How do you think Naomi felt?

- I wonder how Ruth felt traveling to a strange new place. Have you ever traveled to a new place? How did you feel?

- I wonder what the people thought after they saw how God provided for Ruth and Naomi. How does it make you feel to know God cares for you the same way he cared for Ruth and Naomi?

- What do you wonder about our Bible story?

ALPHABET REVIEW

Take a few minutes to go over the letters you have recently learned and the Bible stories that go with them. You can use the coloring pages from each week as a timeline and to aid in reviewing.

OPTIONAL EXTRA ACTIVITIES

KIND OR UNKIND SORTING

WHAT YOU NEED

- Action Sorting Cards, page 143
- Scissors
- Glue

WHAT YOU PREPARE

For each child, make a copy of Action Sorting Cards.

WHAT YOU DO

1. Children cut the picture cards apart. Count cards with the children.

2. Children look at the picture cards and decide whether the action shown is kind or unkind.

3. Assist children to glue the cards in the appropriate boxes.

WHAT YOU SAY

These cards show ways we can show kindness to others. What are some ways you can show kindness at home today?

> **PRESCHOOL SKILLS**
>
> - **Fine-motor skills**
> - **Counting**
> - **Developing empathy**

YOU CAN BE KIND TO OTHERS

WHAT YOU NEED

- Construction paper
- Crayons or markers
- Alphabet stickers

Optional

- Note cards

abc
defghijklmno
pqrstuvwxyz

> **PRESCHOOL SKILLS**
>
> - **Recognizing name in print**
> - **Drawing skills**

WHAT YOU DO

Give each child a piece of construction paper. Children use the letter stickers in order to spell their name at the top of the page. You may wish to write their name on a note card ahead of time for them so they will have something to look at. When they are done with their name, print "can be kind to others" below it. Children finish decorating the page or drawing a picture of a kind action.

GATHERING GRAIN GAME

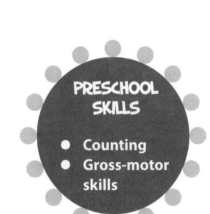

WHAT YOU NEED

- Scraps of yarn, scrap fabric, or shredded paper
- Buckets or baskets, one for each child

WHAT YOU PREPARE

Spread the yarn, fabric, or shredded paper around the room.

WHAT YOU SAY

Remember how Ruth had to go out and gather little bits of grain in order to provide food for her family? We're going to play a game and gather pretend grain!

WHAT YOU DO

1. Children gather up the "grain" and put it into a bucket or basket.
2. Children count the handfuls of grain that they are gathering.
3. When all the grain is gathered, children spread the pretend grain out and play again.

PRESCHOOL SKILLS

- Counting
- Gross-motor skills

HOW MUCH DOES IT WEIGH?

WHAT YOU NEED

- Oats
- Large bowl
- Small paper or plastic cups
- Digital scale (food scale, etc.)

WHAT YOU DO

1. Pour oats into a large bowl and give each child a small paper or plastic cup.
2. Children scoop some oats into their cup and then guess how much it will weigh.
3. Children weigh their cup to see if they are right. Repeat so that each child has a turn.
4. Children also may pour out or add to their cup in order to get to a specific weight.

PRESCHOOL SKILLS

- Estimating
- Pouring
- Exploring sense of touch

R r

R R R R

r r r r

R is for Ruth.

Ruth showed kindness.

R is for Ruth.

Things were looking sad for Naomi and Ruth.
But they knew God would
provide; that was the truth.
Ruth found a field to gather up some food.
Then God gave her a husband,
which really changed the mood!

ACTION SORTING CARDS

Kind Actions

Unkind Actions

S Is for Samson

Judges 13, 16

INTRODUCTION

During the time of the Judges, God chose many unique people to rule over his people. The people were caught in a cycle of sin. Even though God's people turned away from him again and again, God was faithful to raise up a deliverer when the people repented and cried out to him. In the case of Samson, God's people had been held captive by the Philistines for forty years. An angel visited a man and his wife to tell them about Samson's birth. Samson was to abide by certain rules, including never cutting his hair. God would bless Samson with incredible strength and use him to deliver God's people from the Philistines.

OPENING ACTIVITY

FEATS OF STRENGTH

WHAT YOU SAY

Samson was an incredibly strong man. We don't have any record of him performing these feats of strengths, but I bet he could. Let's give them a try!

WHAT YOU DO

1. Children try the following activities:

    - Flamingo—How long can you stand on one leg with no switching?

    - Book Balance—How long can you hold a book straight out in front of you?

    - Staring Contest—How long can you look at someone without blinking?

    - Hopping—How many times can you hop up and down with both feet?

THE BIBLE STORY

Judges 13, 16

God gave a man named Samson special strength in order to defeat people who had captured God's people—the Philistines. Samson had certain rules he had to follow. One rule was to never cut his hair.

Samson was friends with a woman named Delilah. The Philistines asked Delilah to try to figure out the secret of Samson's strength. At first, Samson would not tell her, but finally told her the truth. He explained that his strength came from the Lord and if he cut his hair, his strength would leave him.

Delilah was a trickster. As soon as Samson told her the truth, she cut his hair while he was sleeping. Then, she invited the Philistines (the bad guys!) into the house. Because Samson was no longer strong, they were able to capture him and drag him off to prison.

Samson realized the Lord had left him. He was very sad. After a little while, Samson's hair began to grow back. Samson prayed and asked the Lord to give him strength again. One day, the Philistines brought Samson out so they could make fun of him. They said that their fake god was more powerful than the one true God.

Samson wanted to show everyone who the one true God was. Samson stood in between two pillars of the building. He prayed and asked God for strength. God gave Samson special strength once again and Samson was able to push over the pillars and destroy the entire building and everyone in it. Samson saved God's people by using his special strength.

I WONDER . . .

After the story, read these "wonder" statements and questions out loud to your group. Encourage children to respond.

- I wonder what it was like for Samson to grow up with special strength. Who do you know that is really strong?

- I wonder why Samson did not realize that Delilah was tricking him. What do you think of Delilah trying to trick Samson?

- I wonder what God's people thought after Samson was captured and put in prison. Who is someone you depend on to help you?

- What do you wonder about our Bible story?

ALPHABET REVIEW

Take a few minutes to go over the letters you have recently learned and the Bible stories that go with them. You can use the coloring pages from each week as a timeline and to aid in reviewing.

OPTIONAL EXTRA ACTIVITIES

TEARING PAPER

WHAT YOU NEED

- Scrap paper

WHAT YOU DO

1. Give each child a piece of scrap paper. Children rip the paper in half.

2. **The paper will get stronger when you put more pieces together.** Put two or three pieces together and see if children can still rip the paper in half.

3. Continue in this way, until children can no longer rip the paper.

WHAT YOU SAY

I wonder how many pieces of paper Samson could have ripped at once! Can you guess?

PRESCHOOL SKILLS

- **Gross-motor skills**

HAIR CUT TIME!

WHAT YOU NEED

- Toilet-paper or paper-towel tubes
- Scissors
- Crayons or markers

WHAT YOU PREPARE

If using paper-towel tubes, cut each tube in half. Draw a face on the front of a tube and cut the top into strips. Prepare at least one tube for each child.

WHAT YOU SAY

Imagine this tube person is Samson. I think Samson needs a haircut! In our Bible story, what happened to Samson when his hair was cut?

PRESCHOOL SKILLS

- **Fine-motor skills**
- **Scissor skills**

WHAT YOU DO

1. Children use scissors to trim the "hair" at the top of the roll.

WHERE ARE THE PHILISTINES?

WHAT YOU DO

1. Select a volunteer to be Samson. "Samson" closes their eyes and pretends to be asleep.

2. While Samson is "sleeping", count out loud from one to ten.

3. While you count, the rest of the children hide in the room.

4. When you reach ten, say "Samson, the Philistines are here!"

5. The child pretending to be Samson wakes up and searches for the other children.

6. Select a new volunteer and play as time and interest allow.

PRESCHOOL SKILLS

- Counting
- Playing in groups

NAME SQUARE

WHAT YOU NEED

- Alphabet Squares, page 150
- Scissors
- Construction paper

WHAT YOU PREPARE

Make five copies of Alphabet Squares. Cut the sheets into enough pieces that each child has some letters to cut out. On two or three sheets of construction paper, write the sentences: "Today, we learned about _____. My name is _____."

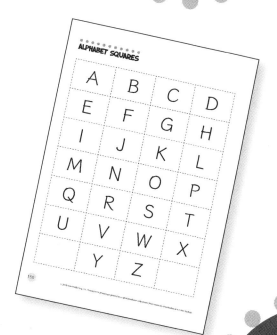

PRESCHOOL SKILLS

- Recognizing their name in print
- Matching letters
- Scissor skills

WHAT YOU DO

1. Children cut out the letters, placing them in the middle of a table.

2. Help children place the correct letters in the blanks to spell Samson's name and then their own. You may wish to write the letters lightly on the paper so they will know where to place their own letters.

S s

S S S S

s s s s

S is for Samson.

Samson was super strong.

COLORING PAGE

S is for Samson.

God made Samson super strong.
And his hair was really long.
His strength was gone when
his hair was shaved.
But God gave it back and the
people were saved.

ALPHABET SQUARES

A	B	C	D
E	F	G	H
I	J	K	L
M	N	O	P
Q	R	S	T
U	V	W	X
	Y	Z	

T Is for Thomas

Matthew 10:2–3, John 20:24–28

INTRODUCTION

People had many expectations for Jesus and his time on Earth. Some of God's people thought that Jesus was going to be a great warrior and overthrow the Roman government. Instead, Jesus was not what people expected at all! To help him in his ministry, Jesus chose twelve disciples. These were ordinary men who may not have stood out in a crowd, but Jesus chose them to spread the good news of the gospel. One disciple, Thomas, was actually a twin! Thomas is famous for doubting that Jesus rose from the dead. He didn't see Jesus when the other disciples did, but Jesus took the time to appear to Thomas as well and help him believe.

OPENING ACTIVITY

IS IT TRUE?

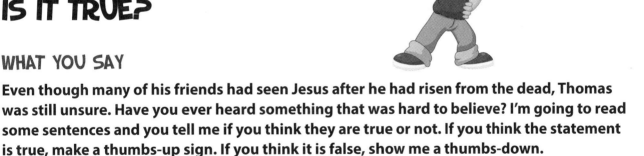

WHAT YOU SAY

Even though many of his friends had seen Jesus after he had risen from the dead, Thomas was still unsure. Have you ever heard something that was hard to believe? I'm going to read some sentences and you tell me if you think they are true or not. If you think the statement is true, make a thumbs-up sign. If you think it is false, show me a thumbs-down.

WHAT YOU DO

1. Read the following sentences. (All are true!)
2. Children guess whether the statements are true or not, making a thumbs-up for true and a thumbs-down for false.
3. Remind children that just because something seems unlikely, it does not mean it's not actually true.
   - Honey does not spoil. If we found some honey from Bible times, we could eat it.
   - A three-year-old was once elected as mayor in Dorset, Minnesota.
   - The blob of toothpaste that sits on your brush is called a *nurdle*.

THE BIBLE STORY

Matthew 10:2–3, John 20:24–28

God sent his Son, Jesus, to Earth to tell us all about the kingdom of God and to save us from our sins. Jesus was born as a baby in Bethlehem and grew up with his earthly parents, Mary and Joseph.

When Jesus was thirty years old, he picked some friends to become his disciples. These men would travel with him, help him, and tell other people about God. The disciples' names were: Simon Peter, Andrew, James son of Zebedee and his brother John, Philip and Bartholomew, Thomas and Matthew the tax collector, James son of Alphaeus, Thaddaeus Simon, and Judas Iscariot.

Jesus told the disciples that he would have to die in order to save the people from the punishment for their sins. He also told them that he would come back to life. This was very hard for the disciples to understand—and believe!

When Jesus did indeed rise again, a few of his disciples saw him. They were amazed! Thomas did not get to see Jesus at first. He wasn't sure if Jesus rising from the dead was really true. Thomas said that unless he saw Jesus for himself, he wouldn't believe.

Jesus did come to see Thomas to show him that he was really alive again. Thomas was amazed. Even though it was hard to believe, we know that with God, all things are possible. Jesus continued to teach his disciples and get them ready to share the good news with others. After Jesus returned to heaven, the disciples continued to tell others about him and all the things he had done.

I WONDER . . .

After the story, read these "wonder" statements and questions out loud to your group. Encourage children to respond.

- I wonder what it was like to be Jesus' special friend, his disciple. You can be a friend to Jesus, too! How does it feel to know you can be a special friend to Jesus?

- I wonder why it was so hard for Thomas to believe Jesus was really alive. Would you have found it hard to believe Jesus was alive again?

- I wonder if the other disciples were upset with Thomas for not believing what they said. Have you ever had a hard time believing something someone told you?

- What do you wonder about our Bible story?

ALPHABET REVIEW

Take a few minutes to go over the letters you have recently learned and the Bible stories that go with them. You can use the coloring pages from each week as a timeline and to aid in reviewing.

OPTIONAL EXTRA ACTIVITIES

DISCIPLE (FOLLOW ME)

WHAT YOU SAY

To be a disciple means to follow someone and do the same things they do. Today, we're going to play a little game to remind us what it means to be a disciple.

WHAT YOU DO

1. Children play a game like Follow the Leader. For the first round, be the leader.

2. Children face the leader. Leader does various movements (jumping up and down, sitting, turning, twirling, etc.) and encourages the children to follow along.

3. After a few minutes, select a volunteer to be the leader, helping the leader as needed.

4. Continue play as time and interest allow.

PRESCHOOL SKILLS

- **Gross-motor skills**
- **Using language to communicate**

DISCIPLE CARDS

WHAT YOU NEED

- Disciple Cards, page 159
- Scissors

Optional

- Laminator

WHAT YOU PREPARE

For each child, make a copy of the Disciple Cards.

OPTIONAL: Laminate Disciple Cards.

WHAT YOU DO

1. Children cut the cards out.

2. Children pair up and play a game of Concentration with the cards. One person in each pair mixes both sets of cards together and then deals all the cards facedown into a grid pattern. Be available to help pairs set up the cards.

3. Players take turns turning over two cards. If the cards match, the player keeps the cards.

4. If the cards don't match, player turns the cards back over.

5. Play continues until all the cards have been matched.

ALTERNATE IDEA: Older children play Go Fish.

PRESCHOOL SKILLS

- Fine-motor skills
- Scissor skills
- Matching like objects
- Using language to communicate

WAS HE A DISCIPLE?

WHAT YOU DO

1. All the children sit on the floor. Read the names listed below.

2. Children stand up if the person was a disciple of Jesus.

3. Children sit down (or remain seated) if the person was not one of the twelve original disciples.

4. Play continues as time and interest allow.

NAMES TO READ:

- Simon Peter (yes)
- Jonah (no)
- Andrew (yes)
- James son of Zebedee (yes)
- Zaccheus (no)
- John, son of Zebedee (yes)
- Adam and Eve (no)
- Philip (yes)
- Bartholomew (yes)
- Thomas (yes)
- The Three Wise Men (no)
- Matthew the tax collector (yes)
- James son of Alphaeus (yes)
- Moses (no)
- Thaddaeus (yes)
- Simon the Zealot (yes)
- Samson (no)
- Judas Iscariot (yes)

PRESCHOOL SKILLS

- Recognizing names
- Gross-motor skills

TWELVE DISCIPLES PORTRAIT

WHAT YOU NEED

- Butcher paper
- Scissors
- Masking tape
- Picture of twelve disciples (find online or in a children's Bible)
- Crayons or markers

WHAT YOU PREPARE

Cut a length of butcher paper long enough to cover a table and tape paper to table.

WHAT YOU SAY

Show the children the picture of the twelve disciples. **Jesus had a lot of close friends. Let's draw a picture of Jesus and his friends. Who are your closest friends? How can you show love to them?**

PRESCHOOL SKILLS

- Using a art tools
- Knowing color words
- Drawing people

WHAT YOU DO

1. Children draw a "group picture" of Jesus with his twelve disciples.

2. As they work, discuss the colors children choose to use.

3. If you have time, write names next to the figures.

ALTERNATE IDEA: If you have the correct number of children and props, children dress up like the twelve disciples. Take a group picture of the class.

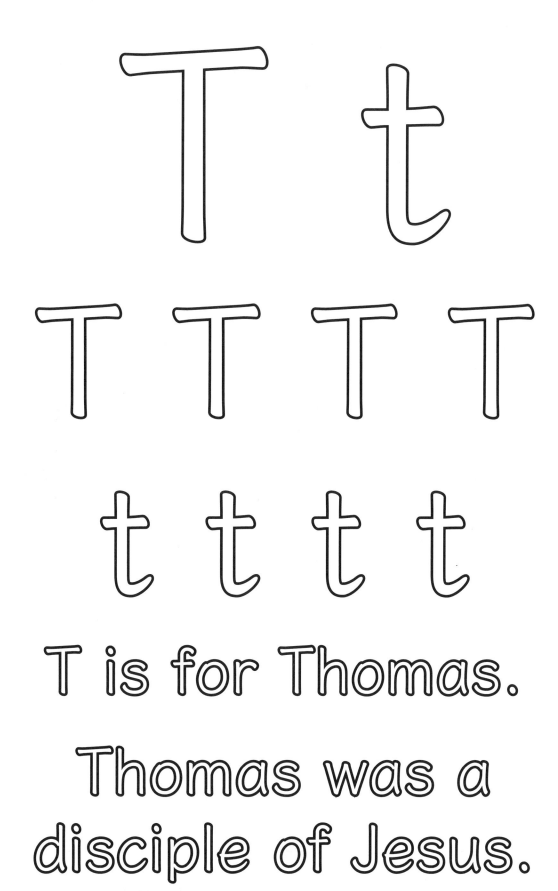

T t

T T T T

t t t t

T is for Thomas.

Thomas was a disciple of Jesus.

T is for Thomas.

Jesus chose twelve men as friends.
On these disciples, he could depend.
Thomas was a disciple who had some doubts.
But Jesus helped him figure it out.

GO FISH DISCIPLE CARDS

Simon Peter	Andrew
James son of Zebedee	John, son of Zebedee
Philip	Bartholomew
Thomas	Matthew
James, son of Alphaeus	Thaddaeus
Simon the Zealot	Judas

U Is for Umbrella

Genesis 6–8

INTRODUCTION

It wasn't long after God created the world that things started to fall apart. It started with Adam and Eve eating the forbidden fruit. Soon, the people on the earth began to turn more and more to their sinful ways and God's heart was deeply troubled (Genesis 6:6). God decided to wipe out all the people on the earth because of their sinfulness. However, one man found favor with God. His name was Noah. God spoke to Noah and told him his plan to destroy the earth and everything in it. God instructed Noah to build a giant boat so that he and his family would be saved. It was an incredible task, but Noah obeyed.

OPENING ACTIVITY

RAINSTORM

WHAT YOU SAY

Have you ever listened to a rainstorm? What kind of sounds do you hear? (Children answer.) **We're going to make some of the same sounds with our bodies.**

WHAT YOU DO

1. Children sit in a circle on the floor.
2. Work together to make the sounds of a storm starting, growing louder, and then moving away.
   - First silently rub your fingers together.
   - Then you rub your two hands together, making a very soft sound.
   - Next you very softly clap your hands together. Then snap your fingers.
   - Now go back to clapping and clap a little louder than you were snapping.
   - Continue to clap louder and then, stomp your feet and clap, making a lot of noise.
   - Now do it in reverse until it is silent again.

160

THE BIBLE STORY

Genesis 6–8

God created the world and everything in it. God created humans and loved them. God wanted to have a relationship with the people that he had made, but they turned their hearts away from him. This made God very sad. He decided to destroy the world and all the people who had chosen to not follow him.

There was one man who loved God—his name was Noah. Noah loved God and obeyed him faithfully. God gave Noah a big job to do. Noah was to build a boat—a giant boat! This giant boat would be called an ark and it would be big enough to hold many animals. Noah and his family would also be able to fit on the ark.

God was planning to send rain on the earth—so much rain, in fact, that the whole earth would be flooded. Noah, his family, and the animals would be safe on the ark. It took Noah a long time to build the ark, and many people did not understand what he was doing. Noah obeyed God anyway.

After the ark was complete and all the animals were on board, God shut the door of the giant boat and it began to rain. It rained for forty days and forty nights. The people did not have umbrellas back then, but I bet they would have used one if they did!

There was so much water from the rain that it covered the entire earth. Once it stopped raining, there was still water on the ground for a long time. Eventually, it dried up and Noah and his family were able to live again on the land.

After they got off the boat, Noah said thank you to God for saving him and his family. God put a rainbow in the sky as a promise that he would never again flood the earth.

I WONDER . . .

After the story, read these "wonder" statements and questions out loud to your group. Encourage children to respond.

- I wonder how long it took for all the animals to get on the ark. What's your guess?
- I wonder what Noah was thinking as he worked hard to build the ark? Say what you think Noah might have been thinking.
- I wonder why the people decided not to obey God. What are some reasons people might choose not to obey?
- What do you wonder about our Bible story?

ALPHABET REVIEW

Take a few minutes to go over the letters you have recently learned and the Bible stories that go with them. You can use the coloring pages from each week as a timeline and to aid in reviewing.

OPTIONAL EXTRA ACTIVITIES

ANIMAL ACTIONS

WHAT YOU NEED

- Animal Cards, page 15
- Scissors

WHAT YOU PREPARE

Make a copy of Animal Cards and cut apart.

WHAT YOU DO

1. Place the cards face down on the table.
2. Have one child pick a card and act out how that animal acts.
   Have the rest of the children try to guess what animal is on the card.
3. Continue playing as time and interest allow.

PRESCHOOL SKILLS

- Group activity

ANIMAL CRACKER SNACK TIME

WHAT YOU NEED

- Animal crackers
- Napkins

WHAT YOU SAY

Remember that Noah brought at least two of every type of animal onto the ark (Genesis 7:2–3). **We can pair up our animals, too!** Talk about the children's favorite animals as they eat their snack.

WHAT YOU DO

1. Give each child a handful of animal crackers and a napkin.
2. Children try to pair up their animal crackers before eating them.

TEACHER TIP: Be sure to post a note for parents about allergies before doing this activity.

PRESCHOOL SKILLS

- Counting
- Matching

RAINBOW IN THE SKY

WHAT YOU NEED

- Remember Rainbow, page 167
- Crayons or markers
- Cotton Balls
- Glue

WHAT YOU PREPARE

For each child, make a copy of Remember Rainbow.

WHAT YOU SAY

Remember whenever you see a rainbow, it is God's promise to never flood the earth again.

WHAT YOU DO

1. Children color the rainbow.
2. When they finish coloring, help them to glue cotton balls onto the clouds to make them fluffy.

TEACHING TIP: You can explain to children what proper rainbow color order is, but don't insist they color according to it. At this age, experimenting with colors and working with crayons or markers is the focus. Talk with children about the colors they choose to use and help them name them.

PRESCHOOL SKILLS

- **Fine-motor skills**
- **Identifying colors**

FIND THE ANIMALS

WHAT YOU NEED

- Various stuffed animals, at least one for each child

WHAT YOU PREPARE

Hide the stuffed animals throughout the room.

WHAT YOU DO

1. Children walk around and try to find one animal.
2. When everyone has found an animal, children gather together.

WHAT YOU SAY

Talk about what kind of animal each child is holding. **What do you think it was like to have that animal on the ark?**

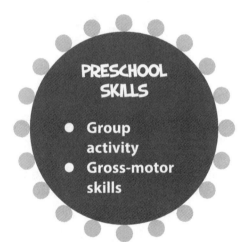

PRESCHOOL SKILLS

- Group activity
- Gross-motor skills

U is for umbrella.

Noah could have used an umbrella.

U is for umbrella.

The rain came down for forty
days from the sky.
Noah did not have an umbrella
to keep him dry.
God gave Noah directions to build a boat.
In this giant ark, Noah and
the animals did float.

REMEMBER RAINBOW

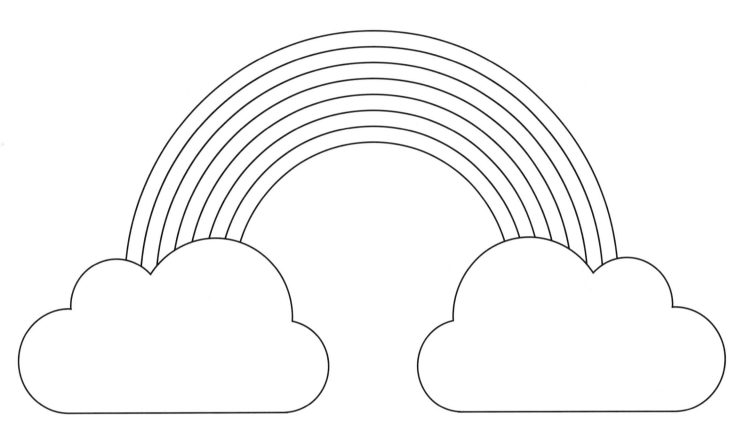

V Is for Victory

Luke 23–24

INTRODUCTION

God sent his son Jesus into the world to save us from our sins. Jesus lived a perfect life and then took the punishment for our sins by dying on the cross. When the soldiers took Jesus down from the cross and placed him a tomb, Jesus friends and disciples were heart-broken. They had heard Jesus say that he would rise again from the dead, but it seemed so hard to believe. Could Jesus really have victory over death?

OPENING ACTIVITY

SO SAD

WHAT YOU NEED

- Tissues

WHAT YOU SAY

Have you ever felt sad? What usually happens when we are sad? (Children respond.) **Sometimes we cry when we are sad. Sometimes we see other people cry when they are sad. What can we do when someone else feels sad?** (Children respond.)

WHAT YOU DO

1. Place a box of tissues on the ground. Children gather in a circle around tissues.

2. One child pretends to be sad and the rest of the children pretends to comfort them, using the tissue if they wish to.

THE BIBLE STORY

Luke 23–24

God created the world and everything in it. God created humans wanted to be friends with them. However, there was sin in the world. When we sin or disobey God, we hurt our relationship with him. God had a plan to take care of the sin in the world.

God sent his Son, Jesus, to the earth. Jesus told people about God and about how much God loved them. Jesus did not sin. He lived a perfect life. That must have been very hard to do! Jesus came to take the punishment for our sins.

When Jesus died on the cross, he paid for all our sins. Because of Jesus' death, we can be forgiven! We can be members of God's family and live with him in heaven forever.

Even though Jesus' death was a sad day for everyone, things did not stay sad for long. Jesus was stronger than death. He had victory over death! Jesus died and was buried, but on the third day, he rose again from the grave.

The women who came to put spices on his body arrived at the tomb, they found the giant stone rolled away. They rushed inside to find Jesus, but he was nowhere to be found! Suddenly, two angels appeared to the women and told them that Jesus had risen! He was no longer dead, but alive. Jesus had victory over death. What good news!

The women (who were friends with Jesus) ran to tell the rest of his followers. His friends and followers were so surprised! Soon, Jesus would visit his disciples and friends so they could all see that he is truly alive.

I WONDER . . .

After the story, read these "wonder" statements and questions out loud to your group. Encourage children to respond.

- I wonder what Jesus' friends were thinking after he died. What do you think they said to each other?
- I wonder how the women felt when they saw the angels outside of the tomb. What would you think if you saw an angel?
- I wonder how Jesus felt to rise again from the dead. Make a face to show how you think Jesus might have felt.
- What do you wonder about our Bible story?

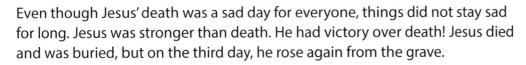

ALPHABET REVIEW

Take a few minutes to go over the letters you have recently learned and the Bible stories that go with them. You can use the coloring pages from each week as a timeline and to aid in reviewing.

OPTIONAL EXTRA ACTIVITIES

SALT DOUGH CROSSES

WHAT YOU NEED

- Salt dough (see recipe at right)
- Cross-shaped cookie cutters
- Rolling pins
- Paper plates
- Marker

SALT DOUGH RECIPE

- 1 cup salt
- 2 cups flour
- ¾ cup water

Mix ingredients together.

WHAT YOU DO

Make a batch of salt dough for the children.

ALTERNATE IDEA: Work together with children to make a batch of salt dough.

WHAT YOU DO

1. Children roll out the dough, cut out cross shapes, and place them on a paper plate. While children work, talk about the sacrifice Jesus made for us on the cross. Write children's names on their paper plates.

2. Set the crosses aside to dry.

3. When the dough is hard, the children can color the crosses with crayons or markers.

PRESCHOOL SKILLS

- Fine-motor skills

JESUS IS ALIVE

WHAT YOU NEED

- Jesus Is Alive Activity Page, page 175
- Alphabet Squares, page 150
- Glue
- Scissors

WHAT YOU PREPARE

For each child, make a copy of Jesus Is Alive Activity Page. For each child, make three copies of Alphabet Squares.

WHAT YOU DO

1. Children to determine the letters the need from Alphabet Squares sheets, and cut them out.

2. Children glue the correct letters into the boxes on Jesus Is Alive Activity Page and color the rest of the page.

ARE YOU ALIVE?

PRESCHOOL SKILLS

- Matching letters
- Fine-motor skills

WHAT YOU NEED

- Bible-times costumes
- Old sheets
- Empty or toy perfume bottles

WHAT YOU PREPARE

Set Bible-times costumes and old sheets in a corner of the room to make a dress-up area.

WHAT YOU DO

1. Children act out the Bible story about Jesus' resurrection. Help children with the story details.

2. After children have acted out the story, they have free play.

PRESCHOOL SKILLS

- Group play
- Listening and remembering a story
- Dramatic play

VICTORY!

WHAT YOU NEED

- Masking tape
- Trash can or bucket
- Soft ball

WHAT YOU PREPARE

Use masking tape to make a starting line at one end of the play area. Set trash can or bucket a few feet away.

WHAT YOU DO

1. Children line up behind the starting line.
2. Children take turns tossing the ball into the trash can or bucket. If they succeed in making it into the bucket, everyone calls out, "Victory!" together.
3. Allow each player up to three tosses to make it into the trash can or bucket.
4. Play continues as time and interest allows..

PRESCHOOL SKILLS

- Gross-motor skills
- Communicating with language
- Taking turns

WHAT YOU SAY

When we say "Victory!" it means that we have won at something. Jesus had victory when he proved he was stronger than death. Many people thought that Jesus was gone forever when he died on the cross, but that's not true. Jesus had victory over death. Jesus is alive!

V is for victory.

Jesus has victory over death.

V is for victory.

Jesus died upon the cross
because of all our sins.
The disciples were sad and wondered
if they'd ever see him again.
Jesus did not stay dead for long.
He had victory, you know!
He rose again and someday,
to heaven we will go.

JESUS IS ALIVE ACTIVITY PAGE

| J | E | S | U | S | | I | S |

| A | L | I | V | E! |

W Is for Water

Matthew 14:22–33

INTRODUCTION

Jesus performed many miracles during his time on Earth, one was his walking on water. He even called Peter out to walk on the water with him. We see clearly the effect of Peter's faith—and also of his doubt—as he steps out of the boat. As long as Peter kept his eyes on Jesus, he remained on top of the water. When Peter started to doubt Jesus, and he sank. Jesus never wavered though. He reached out and rescued Peter. Jesus is powerful. We see this demonstrated again and again through his mighty works on Earth. In faith, we can join Jesus as he continues to show his power throughout the earth today.

OPENING ACTIVITY

WILL IT FLOAT?

WHAT YOU NEED

- Variety of objects (stick, cork, marble, coin, bouncy ball, Lego man, wooden block, pencil, safety pin, etc.)
- Clear container (Fish tank, glass pitcher or bowl, etc.)

WHAT YOU DO

1. Hold up each object. Children guess whether that object will sink or float when you drop it into the water.

2. Drop the object into the water to see if it sinks or floats. Continue until you have used all the objects or as time and interest allow.

WHAT YOU SAY

Sometimes it was very surprising to see what would sink and what would float. In our true story today, we're going to talk about something that stayed on top of the water, even though it didn't seem possible!

THE BIBLE STORY

Matthew 14:22–33

One day, when Jesus was living here on Earth, he told his disciples to get into a boat and cross the lake. Jesus had just finished teaching and feeding a large crowd and he wanted to be able to send the people on their way.

After the people had left, Jesus went up onto a mountain by himself to pray. When evening came, the boat with the disciples in it was in the middle of the lake. The disciples were worried because it was very windy and things on the boat were feeling rocky. Suddenly, the disciples looked up and saw something very strange. It looked like a person was walking on the water! They were very scared!

They disciples did not know it was actually Jesus, walking to them on top of the water! That is incredible. Jesus spoke to the disciples and told them not to be afraid.

One of Jesus' disciples, named Peter, wanted to walk out to Jesus. Jesus encouraged him to come out and Peter got out of the boat and started walking on top of the water just like Jesus was.

At first Peter was doing great, but then he began to be afraid of the strong wind and waves. He began to sink and called out to Jesus. Jesus reached out his hand and saved him. Then, together, they both got back into the boat. When they got into the boat, the wind immediately stopped. The disciples were amazed!

I WONDER . . .

After the story, read these "wonder" statements and questions out loud to your group. Encourage children to respond.

- I wonder what Jesus was praying about on the mountain. What are some things you pray about?
- I wonder how the disciples felt about leaving Jesus behind. What would you have said if you were one of the disciples?
- I wonder how it felt to walk on top of the water. How would you have felt if you were Peter?
- What do you wonder about our Bible story?

ALPHABET REVIEW

Take a few minutes to go over the letters you have recently learned and the Bible stories that go with them. You can use the coloring pages from each week as a timeline and to aid in reviewing.

OPTIONAL EXTRA ACTIVITIES

FOOTPRINTS

WHAT YOU NEED

- Construction paper
- Crayons or markers

WHAT YOU SAY

Why do you think Jesus was able to walk on water? Was it because of special shoes or because he was powerful? (Children respond.) **Today we're going to color tracings of our feet to remember Jesus and Peter walking on the water.**

WHAT YOU DO

1. Trace each child's feet onto a piece of construction paper.
2. Children color in their feet with crayons or markers.

PRESCHOOL SKILLS

- Fine-motor skills

JESUS ON THE WATER

WHAT YOU NEED

- Water Walk, page 182
- Blue tissue paper
- Glue
- Construction paper

WHAT YOU PREPARE

For each child, make a copy of Water Walk. Cut tissue paper into squares.

WHAT YOU DO

1. Children glue the blue tissue-paper squares along the bottom of a piece of construction paper to form a "sea."
2. Children cut the pictures from their copy of Water Walk.
3. Ask children to retell you the story using their picture as a guide.

PRESCHOOL SKILLS

- Fine-motor skills
- Identifying colors
- Remembering and retelling a story

WALKING ON WATER

WHAT YOU NEED

- Gallon-sized resealable plastic bag
- Clear packing tape
- Toy people

WHAT YOU PREPARE

Fill bag with water, seal, and secure with packing tape.

WHAT YOU SAY

Lay the water-filled bag on the table so it spreads out flat. Stand a toy person on the water and talk about how he is "walking on water." **How this is different than what Jesus did?**

WHAT YOU DO

1. Children play with the water-filled bag and toy people.

ALTERNATE IDEAS: You may wish to have more than one bag available. For extra sensory fun, fill the bag with fish confetti and water beads.

PRESCHOOL SKILLS

- Sensory activity
- Using language to communicate

PLANES, TRAINS, AUTOMOBILES, AND BOATS

WHAT YOU NEED

- Several toy versions of transportation (boats, trucks, planes, trains, cars, etc.)

WHAT YOU SAY

Remind children that Jesus was able to walk on the water because he is God. **Jesus is powerful! His friends saw Jesus because they were on a boat. Wherever we go on a boat, in a car, or on a plane, we can remember how powerful Jesus is!**

WHAT YOU DO

1. Children free play with some boats and other types of transportation.

PRESCHOOL SKILLS

- Fine-motor skills
- Identifying colors

W is for water.

Jesus walked on the water.

W is for water.

The disciples got into the boat
and sailed upon the lake.
The wind was strong and soon
they all began to quake.
Jesus walked upon the lake, the
disciples were amazed.
When he calmed the rocky sea,
they gave him all the praise.

X Is for X-Ray

1 Samuel 16

INTRODUCTION

Have you ever quickly formed a first impression of someone only later on to find out you were completely mistaken? It's easy to form opinions of people based on what we can see on the outside. In fact, that's exactly what happened in the Bible story we'll be reading about today. Samuel, a prophet of God, went to the house of Jessie to select a future king for God's people. When the oldest brother, Eliab, walked by, Samuel thought surely this was the next king! But God reminded Samuel, that it is not how a person looks that is important. God was looking for a person who truly loved God. We look at the outside of a person; but like an X-ray, God looks at what's inside the heart.

OPENING ACTIVITY

WHAT IS INSIDE?

WHAT YOU NEED

- Variety of objects (ball, rubber duck, toy man, wooden block, toy horse, plastic flower, shoe, book, etc.)
- Pillowcase

WHAT YOU DO

1. Put an object inside the pillowcase.

2. Children feel the object from the outside and try to guess what it is.

3. When everyone has had a guess, pull the object out of the pillowcase and hold it up for children to see.

4. Repeat with other objects as time and interest allow.

WHAT YOU SAY

Sometimes it was very surprising to see what was actually inside this pillowcase, wasn't it? What do you think would make it easier for us to guess the objects? (Children respond.) Yes! If we could see inside the pillowcase, it would be much easier! Have you ever heard of an X-ray machine? An X-ray can see inside of our bodies. It can see our bones.

In our true story today, we're going to learn about God who can also see inside of us. God can see our thoughts and feelings!

THE BIBLE STORY

1 Samuel 16

Long ago, God's people needed a king. God told a man named Samuel to go and pick out the new king. Samuel went to the house of Jessie to look at all the sons of Jessie. He knew that God had chosen one of these boys to be the next king, but he didn't know which one.

Samuel looked at the sons. The oldest son, Eliab was very tall and handsome. He looked like he would make a great king! But God said to Samuel, "Do not consider how handsome or tall he is. I have not chosen him. The LORD does not look at the things people look at. People look at the outside of a person. But the LORD looks at what is in the heart" (1 Samuel 16:7).

All the sons of Jessie walked in front of Samuel, but God told Samuel again and again the he was not the one that had been chosen. Finally, it looked like there were no sons left! Samuel asked if there was anyone else and Jessie replied that the youngest son, David, was still out in the fields tending the sheep.

They sent for David who came and stood in front of Samuel. God knew that David truly loved him. God told Samuel, "This is the one" (1 Samuel 16:12).

Samuel put oil on David's head and promised that he would someday be king. David continued to love and worship God. It was hard for everyone to understand at first, because David did not seem like a king. However, God cares more about our heart and our love for him than what we look like on the outside.

I WONDER . . .

After the story, read these "wonder" statements and questions out loud to your group. Encourage children to respond.

- I wonder how David's brothers felt when David was chosen as the next king. How would you feel if that happened to someone you know?
- I wonder how David felt knowing he was going to be king. How would you feel if someone said you were going to be king or queen?
- I wonder what God sees when he looks inside you and me. What kinds of thing does God see when he sees what we think and feel?
- What do you wonder about our Bible story?

ALPHABET REVIEW

Take a few minutes to go over the letters you have recently learned and the Bible stories that go with them. You can use the coloring pages from each week as a timeline and to aid in reviewing.

OPTIONAL EXTRA ACTIVITIES

FAMILY PICTURE

WHAT YOU NEED

- White paper
- Crayons or markers

WHAT YOU DO

1. Give each child a piece of paper.
2. Children draw a family picture of David and his family. Jessie had eight sons, including David.
3. Children draw a crown on David's head to show that he would be king someday.

PRESCHOOL SKILLS

- Fine-motor skills
- Remembering details from a story

X-RAY BOOK

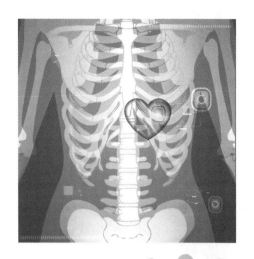

WHAT YOU NEED

- X-rays, real or cartoon (printed from Internet)

Optional

- Story book about X-rays

WHAT YOU SAY

Talk about what an X-ray is and what it can take pictures so doctors can see inside our bodies. **God can see inside of us too, but he's not really interested in our bones. God looks at our heart—our feelings and the things we love. What does God see when he looks inside of your heart? What do you love?**

WHAT YOU DO

1. Children explore X-rays and books.

OPTIONAL: Read a story book about X-rays to the children.

PRESCHOOL SKILLS

- Remembering and retelling a story
- Using language to communicate
- Understanding how to hold a book properly
- Understanding that text has meaning

GOD LOOKS AT THE HEART

WHAT YOU NEED

- Heart hole punch (available at most craft stores)
- Construction paper in various colors
- Crayons or markers
- Glue

WHAT YOU PREPARE

Using the hole punch, cut out several hearts from construction paper, at least ten hearts per child. On a separate sheet of construction paper, print the sentence, "God sees inside my heart."

WHAT YOU DO

1. Children glue the hearts onto a piece of construction paper. Talk with kids about the colors of the hearts.
2. Children copy "God sees inside my heart" across the bottom of the page.

PRESCHOOL SKILLS

- Fine-motor skills
- Identifying shapes
- Identifying colors

INSIDE MY BODY

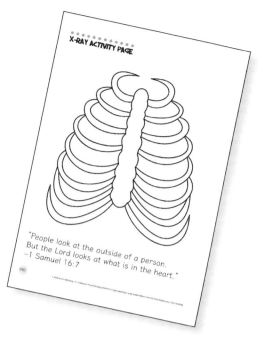

WHAT YOU NEED

- X-Ray Activity Page, page 190
- Scissors
- Crayons or markers
- Heart-shaped stickers

WHAT YOU PREPARE

For each child, make a copy of X-Ray Activity Page.

WHAT YOU DO

Children cut out the heart, color the rib cage, and then place a heart sticker in place.

WHAT YOU SAY

Remind children that God can see all of us, even the thoughts and feelings we have inside. Describe the various parts of the body including the bones inside that we can see with an X-ray machine.

PRESCHOOL SKILLS

- Understanding the body
- Fine-motor skills

X is for X-ray.
God can see inside
our heart.

X is for X-ray.

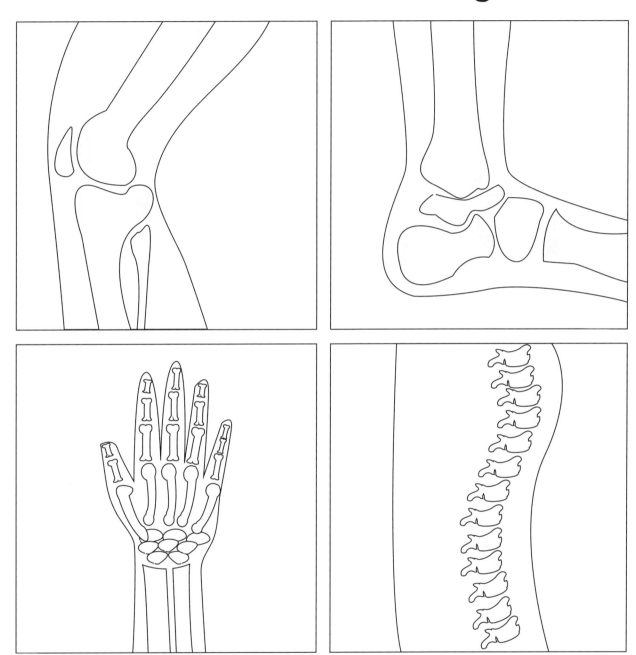

God's people needed a brand-new king.
One who would try to do the right thing.
David was a boy who loved the Lord.
He became the king and was adored.

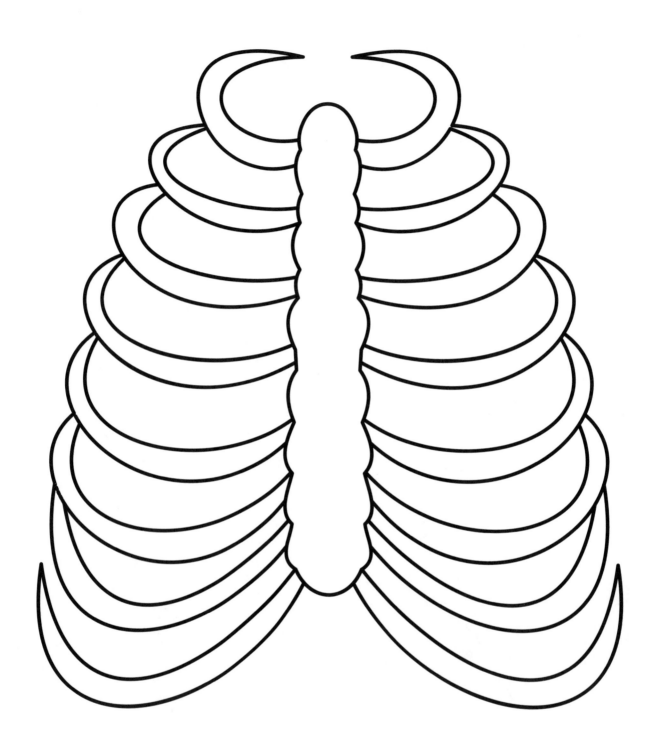

"People look at the outside of a person.
But the Lord looks at what is in the heart."
−1 Samuel 16:7

Y Is for Young King Josiah

2 Kings 22–23

INTRODUCTION

So often, we ask children what they want to be when they grow up, forgetting that children can get a lot accomplished while they are still young! In our true story today, we read about a boy who became king when he was just eight years old. He reigned in Jerusalem for thirty-one years and he followed God. In the eighteenth year of King Josiah's reign, when he was twenty-six years old, Josiah decided to repair God's temple, which had fallen into disrepair. When work was being done on the temple, some scrolls were found inside! When the scrolls were read, King Josiah realized he had not fully been obeying God! He decided to change his ways right away and the Lord was very pleased with his actions.

OPENING ACTIVITY

HOW TALL ARE YOU?

WHAT YOU NEED

- Measuring tape
- Piece of paper

WHAT YOU DO

1. Using the measuring tape, measure the height of each child.
2. Write down the children's names and heights on the paper.

WHAT YOU SAY

The average eight-year-old is about fifty inches tall. Use measuring tape to show the children how tall fifty inches is. **Remember, Josiah was only eight years old when he became king.**

THE BIBLE STORY

2 Kings 22–23

Josiah was eight years old when he became king. He did the right thing and tried his best to follow God.

When Josiah was twenty-six, he had been king for eighteen years and he decided to make repairs to God's temple. The temple was where God's people went to worship him. Josiah picked out workers and gave them money to fix things up and make the temple nice again.

While the workers were busy cleaning and fixing up the temple, someone found a book. It was the book of the law. King Josiah had it read aloud. He realized he had not been following God's laws! He was very upset. He decided to make some changes in his kingdom.

God saw King Josiah's response and was very pleased. He promised he would not bring disaster to the kingdom while Josiah was still the king. King Josiah gathered his people together and read to them all God's words. The king explained the changes he was going to be make in the kingdom. The people agreed to follow God!

King Josiah knocked down statues of fake gods and idols and took away all the altars dedicated to fake gods. The king told the people to celebrate God's Passover and warned them not to worship fake gods. Neither before nor after Josiah was there a king like him who turned to the LORD as he did—with all his heart and with all his soul and with all his strength.

I WONDER . . .

After the story, read these "wonder" statements and questions out loud to your group. Encourage children to respond.

- I wonder what it was like to be such a young king. Would you want to be a king or queen? Why?
- I wonder what kinds of things you would do if you were king or queen. What do you think?
- I wonder how the people felt when they heard God's commands being read. What commands from God do you know?
- What do you wonder about our Bible story?

● ● ● ● ● ● ● ● ● ●

ALPHABET REVIEW

Take a few minutes to go over the letters you have recently learned and the Bible stories that go with them. You can use the coloring pages from each week as a timeline and to aid in reviewing.

OPTIONAL EXTRA ACTIVITIES

CLEANING UP THE TEMPLE

WHAT YOU NEED

- Child-safe cleaning supplies (washcloths or paper towels, feather duster, broom, etc.)

WHAT YOU SAY

Remember, Josiah was working to clean up the temple when he found God's special book. We can clean up our room!

WHAT YOU DO

1. Children the cleaning supplies to clean up the room.
2. In addition to using supplies, they can put things away.

PRESCHOOL SKILLS

- **Gross-motor skills**
- **Remembering details in a story**

KNOCKING DOWN THE IDOLS

WHAT YOU NEED

- Blocks

WHAT YOU SAY

Set up the blocks in a tower. **In King Josiah's lifetime, people would build statues and then worship them like they were a god. We know there is only one true God and King Josiah knew it, too. That's why Josiah knocked down all the statues. Let's build towers and knock them down!**

WHAT YOU DO

1. Children knock down your tower of blocks.
2. Assist children to rebuild the tower and then knock down again.
3. Play continues as time and interest allow.

PRESCHOOL SKILLS

- **Stacking blocks**
- **Following instructions**
- **Motor skills**
- **Using hand-eye coordination**

BUILDING A TEMPLE

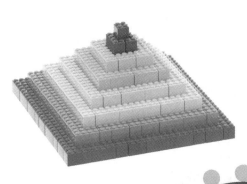

WHAT YOU NEED

- Building blocks (Lincoln Logs, Legos, Duplo Blocks, etc.)

WHAT YOU SAY

Josiah didn't have to build a temple from nothing, but there were a lot of repairs that needed to be made. Let's build temples!

WHAT YOU DO

1. Children use building blocks to build a temple.

PIN THE CROWN ON THE KING

WHAT YOU NEED

- Josiah's Crown, page 197
- Scissors
- Masking tape

WHAT YOU PREPARE

Make enough copies of Josiah's Crown so that there is one crown for each child. Cut out crowns and attach a loop of masking tape to the back of each crown.

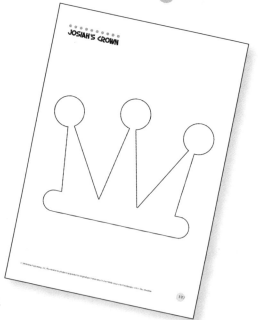

WHAT YOU DO

1. Children play a game like Pin the Tail on the Donkey.

2. Select a volunteer to be the "King."

3. The other children take turns closing their eyes, walking to the King, and trying to stick a crown on the King's forehead.

4. When all the children have had a turn, select a new volunteer and play again as time and interest allow.

Y is for young
King Josiah.

Young King Josiah
loved God.

Y is for young King Josiah.

Josiah became a king when
he was very young.
He followed God's ways, to God he clung.
He realized his people were not
following God's ways.
He changed things around and
obeyed for all his days.

 Z Is for Zacchaeus

Luke 19:1–10

INTRODUCTION

Jesus was an amazing person. Everywhere he went, crowds of people would gather around Jesus. It was hard to get close to him, and for some people—it was hard to even get a glimpse of him! Zacchaeus was a man who wanted to see Jesus. The trouble was, Zacchaeus was very short and couldn't see over the crowds. So he did something a little crazy. Zacchaeus climbed up into a tree to see Jesus. As Jesus passed by, he noticed Zacchaeus in the tree and spoke to him. Jesus invited himself over to Zacchaeus' house and Zacchaeus gladly accepted!

OPENING ACTIVITY

IT'S CROWDED IN HERE!

WHAT YOU NEED

- Rope

WHAT YOU DO

1. Form a circle on the ground with the rope. Children stand inside the circle.

2. On your signal, children jump out of the circle.

3. Make the circle a little smaller and have children step back inside.

4. Continue in this pattern, making the circle smaller and more "crowded" until the children no longer fit in the circle.

WHAT YOU SAY

Have you ever been in a very crowded place? What was it like? How do you think Zacchaeus felt trying to get through the crowds to see Jesus?

THE BIBLE STORY

Luke 19:1–10

When Jesus lived here on Earth, he often traveled from town to town. One day, Jesus was passing through Jericho. A man named Zacchaeus was there. He wanted to see Jesus. Zacchaeus was very wealthy, but he wasn't liked very much.

Zacchaeus wanted to see who Jesus was, but because he was short he could not see over the crowd. So, he ran ahead and climbed a sycamore tree to see him. When Jesus got close to the tree, he looked up and said to him, "Zacchaeus, come down at once. I must stay at your house today" (Luke 19:5). So Zacchaeus came down at once and gladly welcomed Jesus to his home.

The other people of Jericho saw this and began to mutter. They did not like Zacchaeus because he cheated them out of their money. They could not believe that Jesus wanted to be friends with a person like that. The people forgot that Jesus loves everyone.

After Jesus went to Zacchaeus' house, Zacchaeus realized he had been doing wrong. He told Jesus, "Right now I will give half of my possessions to the poor. If I have cheated anybody I'll pay them back four times the amount I took."

Jesus was very pleased to hear Zacchaeus say these things. Jesus knew that it was important to spend time with people who did not love God yet. He was glad that Zacchaeus decided to follow God and do the right thing.

I WONDER . . .

After the story, read these "wonder" statements and questions out loud to your group. Encourage children to respond.

- I wonder why Zacchaeus wanted to see Jesus so badly. Why do you think he wanted to see Jesus?
- I wonder how Zacchaeus felt when Jesus said he would go to Zacchaeus' house. How would you feel if someone important came to your house?
- I wonder why Zacchaeus decided to pay back the people he'd cheated. Have you ever made up for doing something wrong?
- What do you wonder about our Bible story?

ALPHABET REVIEW

Take a few minutes to go over the letters you have recently learned and the Bible stories that go with them. You can use the coloring pages from each week as a timeline and to aid in reviewing.

OPTIONAL EXTRA ACTIVITIES

WHAT KIND OF TREE IS IT?

WHAT YOU NEED

- Various leaves
- Tree and leaf identification book (check your local library or you online for "common leaf identification chart")

WHAT YOU SAY

Talk about how each leaf come from different trees. **Remember Zacchaeus climbed up in a tree to see Jesus. Do you remember what kind of tree Zacchaeus climbed? It was a sycamore!**

WHAT YOU DO

1. Spread the leaves out on the table as children look at them.
2. Look together at the book or chart and match the leaves to their proper tree.

Teaching Tip: Take a nature walk with the children to gather the leaves needed for this activity.

PRESCHOOL SKILLS

- Matching objects
- Remembering details from a story

FIND THE COINS

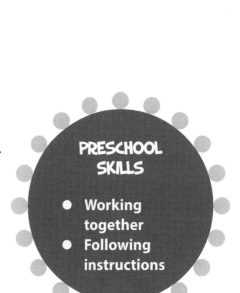

WHAT YOU NEED

- Gold or silver paper plates, one for each child (available at party stores)
- Marker
- Index cards

WHAT YOU PREPARE

Number each plate, printing large numbers on the plates. Hide the plates around the room.

WHAT YOU SAY

Zacchaeus loved money and probably had a lot of gold (or silver) coins. Let's search our room for coins!

WHAT YOU DO

1. Give a numbered index card to each child.
2. Children search to find the plate with the matching number.
3. When everyone has found their plates, they hide plates in the room again.
4. Assign new numbered index cards to the children and play again.
5. Continue play as time and interest allow.

ALTERNATE IDEAS: Children count the plates, line up plates in number order, etc.

PRESCHOOL SKILLS

- Working together
- Following instructions

UP IN A TREE

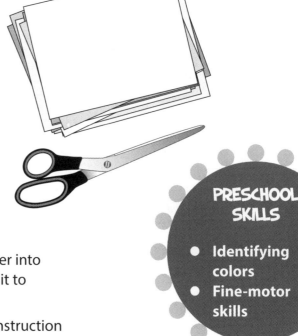

WHAT YOU NEED

- Scissors
- Brown construction paper
- Glue
- White construction paper
- Green tissue or construction paper
- Crayons or markers

WHAT YOU DO

1. Children cut the brown construction paper into wide rectangles for a tree trunk and glue it to a sheet of white construction paper.

2. Children rip the green tissue paper or construction paper into small pieces and glue them onto the top of the trunk to represent trees.

3. Children can draw Zacchaeus in the tree, Jesus at the bottom of the tree, or both!

PRESCHOOL SKILLS
- Identifying colors
- Fine-motor skills

NAME GAME

WHAT YOU NEED

- What's Your Name, page 205
- Crayons or markers

WHAT YOU SAY

Zacchaeus had a very interesting name! You all have great names, too. Let's practice writing our names on each other's pages.

WHAT YOU PREPARE

For each child, make a copy What's Your Name? Sheet.

PRESCHOOL SKILLS
- Recognizing their name in print
- Writing first name

WHAT YOU DO

1. Children write their names on each other's papers.

2. If there are too many papers to sign or if children are having difficulty—children write their name on one paper and then practice reading the names together.

ALTERNATE IDEA: If children are very young, encourage them to print the first letter of their names.

Z z

Z Z Z Z

Z Z Z Z

Z is for Zacchaeus. Zacchaeus climbed a tree.

Z is for Zacchaeus.

Zacchaeus heard that Jesus
was coming to his town.
He wanted to see him, but he was
too close to the ground.
Zacchaeus was a short man, so
he climbed up in a tree.
When Jesus walked by and spoke,
it filled his heart with glee.

WHAT'S YOUR NAME? SHEET

Write your name on a line below

_____

_____

_____

_____

_____

Index

MORE ROSEKIDZ BOOKS FROM LINDSEY WHITNEY

CHECK OUT THESE GREAT TITLES:

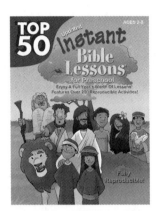

Teach the best 50 lessons from the popular Instant Bible Lessons series. The Top 50 Instant Bible Lessons for Preschoolers includes quick and easy-to-use resources for Sunday-school teachers with reproducible hand-outs, arts and crafts templates, puzzles, games, and step-by-step instructions. Ages two to five years.

ISBN-13: 9781628624977

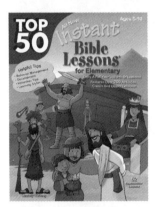

More great lessons from the popular Instant Bible Lessons series. *The Top 50 Instant Bible Lessons for Elementary* includes the same types of resources for Sunday-school teachers as our preschool book: reproducible hand-outs, arts and crafts templates, puzzles, games, and step-by-step instructions. Ages five to ten years.

ISBN-13: 9781628624984

The RoseKidz Top 50 series continues with the *Top 50 Memory Verse Lessons*. Memory verses are vital to hiding God's Word in the heart and mind of every child. This book is packed with fun, interactive, creative, and engaging ways to get children excited about memorizing Scripture. The 50 verses are in an easy-to-learn format. Ages five to ten.

ISBN-13: 9781628625059

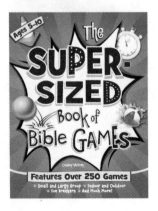

This *Super-Sized Book of Bible Games* is a giant, HUMONGOUS book packed with over 250 exciting games for every occasion. Each game has an overview, step-by-step instructions, supply list, Scripture connection, discussion questions, and a teachable moment connecting God's Word to the activity. Find exactly what you need with its quick and convenient index arranged by topic, type, and Scripture.

ISBN-13: 9781628625462